ONE WORLD OF FASHION

by
M. D. C. Crawford

Third Edition Revised and Edited by
Beatrice Zelin and Josephine Ellis Watkins

FAIRCHILD PUBLICATIONS, INC.
NEW YORK

Third Edition, Copyright   1967
Second Edition, Copyright   1955
First Edition, Copyright   1946
Fairchild Publications, Inc., New York

Library of Congress Catalog Card Number: 67-15747

Printed in the United States of America

ONE WORLD OF FASHION

Contents

PLATES

Foreword

One World of Fashion by the late M.D.C. Crawford has been influential in the field of Fashion Research. Mr. Crawford's depth of appreciation of sources of inspiration from all geographic areas of the world and his wealth of knowledge of the history and the development of fabric and apparel have given important stimulus and information both to the tyro and to the recognized professional in the field of fashion.

In his introduction, M.D.C. Crawford states that "(Fashion) is a never-ending cycle of renewal and growth. It has been continuous throughout the ages. It is 'One World of Fashion'." With this statement the present authors heartily agree. They are honored to have been requested to supply supplemental material on fashion development from 1943 through 1966 in the reprinting of *One World of Fashion.*

Within the last twenty years, the fashion business has developed into a giant industry within the United States of America. It ranks third in the economy of the country and produces a gross product of more than fifteen billion dollars. From small unit firms it has grown into large plants whose shares are listed on the stock exchange. Our mode of living and system of transportation have emphasized whole new areas of living: suburbia; travel by air, sea, land; vacations in spring, summer, fall, and winter. Rapid communications; new channels of distribution; and merchandising techniques of advertising, publicity, and display have promoted more rapid changes of fashion. Research studies in the textile field have provided a wealth of new fabrics which have stimulated designers to create new structures, cuts, and handling. Emphasis on easy care has influenced use of synthetic combinations and of paper and stretch fabrics. The American garment industry is recognized by the world as the leading authority on specialization and mass production.

With all of the development in technology and scientific method, the designer remains the most important factor in keeping fashion a dynamic art as a reflection of our current mores. An awareness of past civilizations and an alertness to the needs and tempo of the present are necessary for any creator of ideas.

The authors have decided that it would be appropriate to limit their discussion to the outstanding American designers of the past twenty years. This follows Mr. Crawford's report on the "Renaissance of Fashion 1942" which was an attempt to promote and to recognize American designers. In no way is this a reflection on the contributions of the foreign designers. In fact we are more than ever "One World" and interdependent. There is more interchange of ideas between Europe and America and between America and Europe than ever before. All have something to contribute. It is our belief, with Mr. Crawford, that "culture joins all mankind in a common heritage of beauty; and men, in all times and under all conditions of life, have produced ornaments and decorations."

JOSEPHINE ELLIS WATKINS
Director of Community Resources and
Professor of Apparel Design

BEATRICE ZELIN
Assistant Director of Placement and
Professor of Apparel Design

March, 1967

ONE WORLD OF FASHION

All art was once Fashion. Art and Fashion are separated only by the element of time. Any art may become an inspiration for Fashion. It is a continuous process of ideas, techniques and interpretations.

For almost a half of a century, *Women's Wear Daily* published pages of sketches dealing with the fabric and costume arts of many lands and many ages, and in some instances, interpretative drawings of their use at various periods of American style. They began this practice during the fashion emergencies of World War I, and continued it because it seemed to fit into the needs of the professional designers.

Fashion may be the whim of the moment, an expression of the transient desires and aspirations of a season or a few brief years, but, it is composed of constantly renewed elements, which are more ancient than any written history. The arts of ancient civilizations have influenced and molded the modes of our modern world. The achievements of the ancient crafts reflecting the great traditions of the past are sources of constant inspirations and of research study for the development of new fashions or for new forms of art. With the spread of machine production these peasant and tribal arts are becoming part of a vanishing culture. Our museums are the custodians of these treasures reflecting man's creative accomplishments.

No conception of fashion can be complete unless it includes something more than the costumes themselves. We should know something about jewelry, millinery, and footwear, the art of lace making, weaving, knitting and embroidery. We should never think of these forms of expression as static and unchanging, but, rather as factors of energy constantly renewing themselves and taking new forms.

This publication is intended to be a part of the working equipment of the designer, and as a basic guide for broader research, rather than as a reference work or a chronicle of the modes. *Women's Wear Daily* pioneered in the establishment of those intimate relationships among designers, stylists and museum collections.

Culture joins all mankind in a common heritage of beauty; and men, in all times and under all conditions of life, have produced ornaments and decorations, and those qualities we call "The Arts." All of these arts were, at one time or another, contemporaneous fashion. It is a never ending cycle of renewal and growth. It has been continuous throughout the ages. It is "One World of Fashion".

M.D.C. CRAWFORD

January, 1946

PLATES

Fashion in the Ancient Near East

The most ancient civilizations, and the most ancient arts, come to us from the ruined and almost forgotten cities of the lower Euphrates valley. Sumerians, Assyrians, Babylonians, Akkadians, Medes and Persians carried this story from 3500 B. C. to the conquests of Persia by Alexander the Great in the year 325 B.C. Draped costumes of wool, embroidered, fringed and pleated, are shown in the cylinder seals of Sumer. The patterns of embroidery remain for us in the beautiful stone carvings of Susa and Persepolis.

The Assyrian bas-relief of the god-like king with wings shows the draper's art, and the rich textures, of about 700 B.C.

The costume of the Royal Archer of Nineveh, in the lion hunt, shows, not only stone carving at its height, but also indicates some very interesting details of costume design.

In the center, on the right hand side is the famous bas-relief of Saphur I, and, kneeling before him, is the Roman Emperor, Valerian, whom he defeated. The King of the Medes wears a sort of trousers.

The bottom band shows Persian conquerors bringing subject peoples before the king. The trousered figures are believed to have been representatives of the Mongol or Scythian race from central Asia.

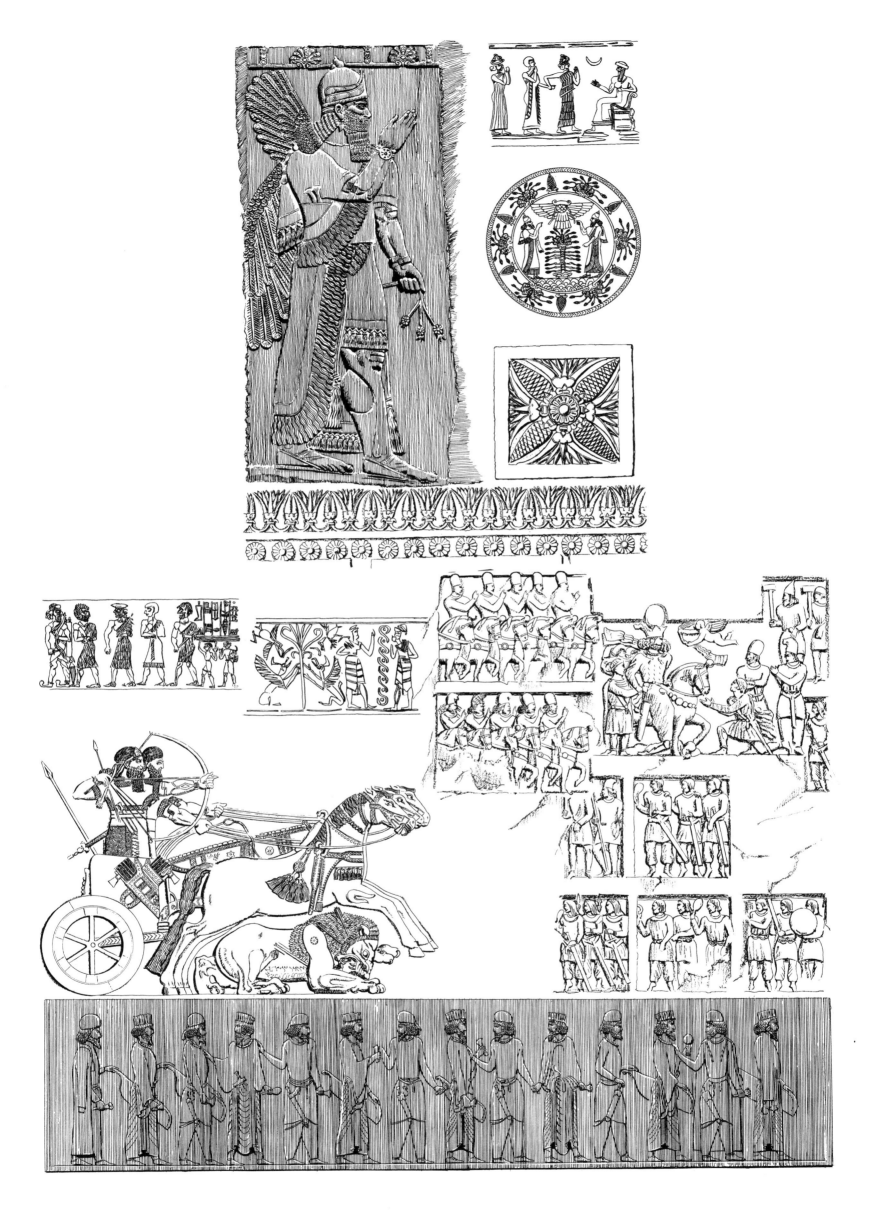

Fashions of the Ancient Nile

Egypt was the historic land of linen. No linens have ever been produced in any other part of the world which compare in lightness and fineness with those webs which Egypt knew two thousand years before our era. The semi-transparent fabric first appears in fashion along the Nile. But, linen was difficult to dye, so Egypt sought her color satisfaction in bead work, in jewels and flowers.

The jeweled headdress, on the right hand side of the illustration, was made of gold and lapis lazuli. The figures of the two hawks below it is a pectoral ornament worn in Egypt almost four thousand years ago.

On the left is a carved figure of a man wearing a kilt, and below him is a wall painting of a Libyan prisioner wearing an interesting kind of robe.

Ancient Jewelry and Modern Fashion

Personal ornament is far older than any costume design expressed in fabric. It begins in magic and in symbolism, in amulets and charms. Rings, earrings, necklaces and hair ornaments are still worn by many primitive people to protect them from evil spirits. Jewelry is worn today to protect the well-dressed woman from monotony in costume. Many forms of modern costumes are specifically designed with jewelry in mind.

Jewelry was made in the valley of the Euphrates five thousand years ago which might easily be fashionable today. The same is true of the ancient ornaments recovered from the graves of Egypt, India, China, Persia, Constantinople, Peru and Chile.

Some years ago the Metropolitan Museum of Art presented an exhibition, "The House of Jewels," in which five thousand years of the history of precious ornament was placed on display. We have included, in this illustration, many of the outstanding examples of this exhibition, together with other and comparable forms of expression from the ancient arts of South America.

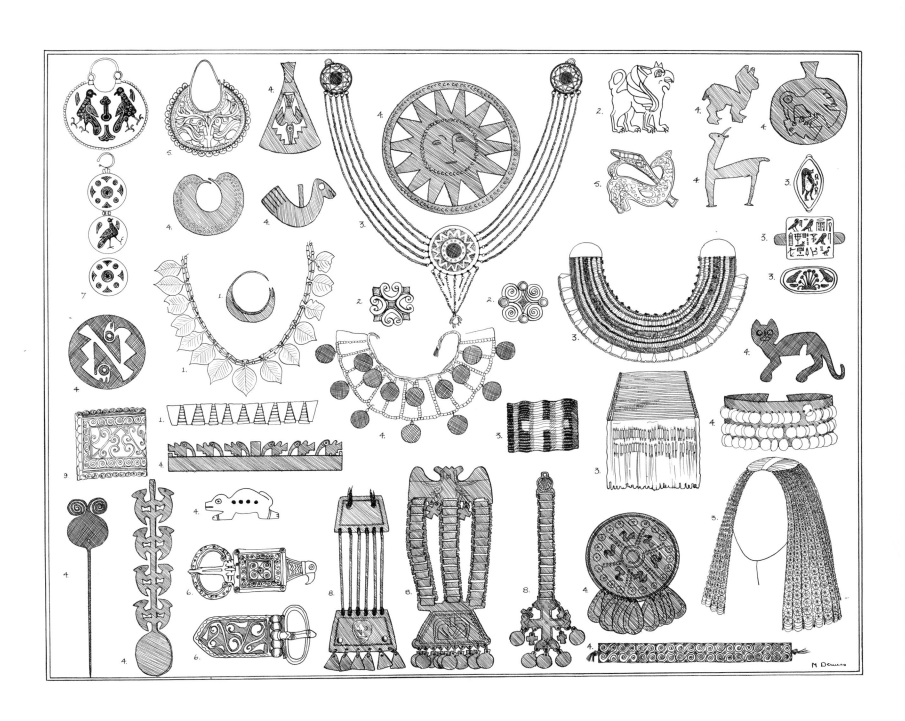

What Do the Merchants Bring — Trade and Culture

International commerce is of very ancient origin. The islands of Java, Sumatra, and Borneo, and the Molukka Islands (The Spice Islands), were first discovered and settled by the Hindu navigators sailing out of the ports of the Indus River, and these same islands were later discovered by the Chinese junks sailing from the south of China. Mesopotamia, Egypt, India and the islands of Cyprus and Crete formed a pattern of trade perhaps 3000 years before the Christian Era. The first European to open this trade to western navigation was Vasco da Gama. Early in the 15th Century, he sailed around the Cape of Good Hope. As he came to the ports of the Red Sea and Arabia, he was quick to recognize the fact that the Hindus and Arabic sailors had already solved the navigation of these seas, and sailed eastward on one monsoon, collected their merchandise in the ports of the Orient, and sailed back to the mouth of the Red Sea on the reverse monsoon. Long before that time, trade had swept from port to port along the coast of the Red Sea, the Arabian peninsula and the far side of India and Ceylon.

Phoenicia was a Greek word meaning "Land of Purple," and the Phoenicians were famous for their purple fabrics. They were a maritime people from the Persian Gulf who, about 3000 B.C., had come to the coast of the Mediterranean and, under their great King Hiram, furnished the luxuries used in King Solomon's temple.

In the early part of the 1st Century, Hippalus discovered the secret of sailing across on the monsoon, and an adventurous navigator-merchant, probably from the port of Berenice on the Red Sea, wrote, a little later, our first commercial account of these voyages, describing the character of the people in each of the ports touched on by the hardy sailors and the kinds of merchandise available. "The Periplus of the Erythraen Sea" was originally written in Ptolemaic Greek, and it has been translated with copious notes and comments by Wilfred H. Schoff. In the account of this trade, mention is made of such luxuries as tortoise-shell, ivory, undressed cloth from Egypt; robes from Arsinoe, where the Suez Canal runs today; Indian cotton cloth; girdles; coats of skin; muslin; finished cloth; various perfumery essences; purple cloths; clothing in the Arabian style, with sleeves embroidered or woven with gold; pearls; purple dyes; figured linen; silk yarn indigo dyed; fine, lightweight muslins woven in the valleys of the Ganges; silk; silk yarn and silk cloth. In other words, a fine specialty shop of today could be furnished with the different types of merchandise which these ancient galleys brought into Europe from the Far East. This list indicates that the origin of the luxuries we still delight in is very ancient indeed, and the changes have been in detail rather than in basic commodities ever since.

In the countries touched on by this ancient trade, conservatism reigns, and many of the costumes worn by the natives of these countries today have changed only slightly in detail from what they must have been when the first navigator-merchants saw them three or four thousand years ago. At one time, Rome was the greatest empire for these luxuries and, from time to time, discoveries of Roman coins are still made in the ruins of India and the Far East. The whole subject is discussed in Revelations with reference to the burning of Rome in 63 A.D. "Alas, alas, that great city wherein were made rich all that had ships in the sea by reason of her costliness . . . for thy merchants were the great men of the earth."

Cochin
China

Afghanistan

Coptic

Siam

Borneo

India

Ceylon

Persia

Turkey

Ceylon

Hainan
Islands

Java — A Living Museum of the Ancient Arts of India and China

Java is a living museum of the fabric and costume arts of ancient India and China. The chief element of the population is Malay, a maritime people who came from southern Asia between the 1st and 8th Centuries of our era. They brought with them, among their great arts, cotton culture, and the technique of wax resist dyeing, or batik, and the draped costume of southern India. At about the same time, Chinese merchants introduced loose trousers, and a livelier idea of color and pattern; and a still later immigration of Mohammedan Malays, in the 14th Century, brought with them certain elements of Persian tailored costumes and tinsel weaves.

The Portuguese, Dutch, and English arrived as traders in the 16th Century; the Dutch remained as rulers.

Java, with her population of 63 million, (including Madura, a small island off N.E. Java) 98% of which are purely Oriental in blood and tradition, has retained their rich and stimulating arts as an inspiration for modern times.

Persia — An Ancient Art that Is Always New

The Persian arts from the 12th to the 16th Centuries live vividly for us in the brilliant colors and spirited drawings of her glazed pottery. It is from these bowls and tiles that we gain our most perfect impression of what her ancient fabric arts must have been. Here there is no fading, nor change of colors. Persian art carries on the rich traditions of Mesopotamia, Babylonia and Assyria. It preserves for us the great traditions of a distinguished past and keeps alive the colors and designs that are older than any living nation.

Through the Arab Conquests and the Crusades, these arts spread to Sicily, Spain and to Italy and left a Persian impression on the great Italian Renaissance. Many of these conceptions of designs still live in the silks of Lyons.

From time to time, modern artists will find a great refreshment by going back to early Persian originals and seeking inspiration at the source.

Tinsel Fabrics from Alexander the Great to Lyons

Alexander the Great described tinsel fabrics in 327 B.C. as he found them in Central Asia. But these arts were already ancient in the Near East. Alexander's conquests are all but forgotten, but gold and silver tinsel yarns still decorate fabrics.

For centuries the city of Ahmadabad, in northern India, has been a center of the textile arts. She gathered her inspiration from southern India, from ancient Persia and the influence of trade with China. Down to the middle of the 19th Century she still was making fabrics in silk and cotton, and gold and silver tinsel yarns. They represent not only a high degree of present skill in loom work, but contain the traditions of loveliness of many forgotten centuries.

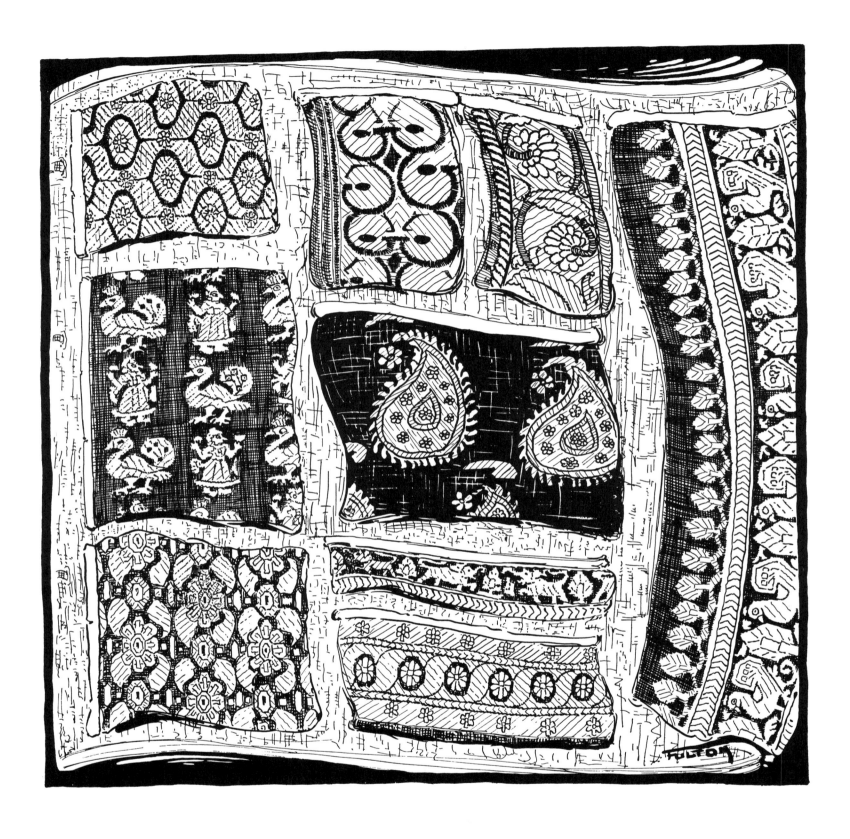

A Thing of Beauty Is a Joy Forever

Japan borrowed from China paper, silk culture and the idea of the stencil. Japanese craftsmen carried the art of the stencil to an equisite degree of physical and artistic perfection. The stencils were used with a resist-paste made from wild rice starch. This art is undoubtedly the parent of modern film printing. A collection of Japanese stencils should offer to the modern designer of film prints an inexhaustable supply of ideas.

The craftsmen who produced these stencils belonged neither to the Samurai nor to any of the military castes which once ruled and ultimately ruined the Japanese Empire. Art has an Empire of its own.

All arts of all peoples are the heritage of all artists capable of understanding and interpreting them. Beauty has nothing whatever to do with the memory of those bitter days which are passed.

The Far East Used Knots instead of Buttons

The ornamental knot, in many intricate forms, is used in Chinese and Japanese costumes to perform the same function as the button and the toggle in the costumes of Europe. Buttons do exist in ancient China, but they are always copies in metal, ivory or jade of knots, and they are caught in loops rather than in button-holes. Buttons are practically non-existent in early Japan, and there is no Japanese word for button.

Ornamental knots are used, not only for costumes, but on boxes and in various other containers, and for ceremonial purposes. For each occasion, there is a special knot, and the form of the knot is regulated by precise and rigid traditions. They were a part of the court etiquette.

In 1762, this information was gathered together by Ise Teijo of the Shogun's Court and the book remained in manuscript until it was printed in 1840.

Special knots were used in ceremonial costumes of the Shogun's Court to denote social rank and official position. There were knots for both the long and the short swords, for whips, umbrellas, food, writing and toilette boxes, and for many other purposes. These knots were given fanciful names; the dragonfly, the butterfly, the plum, the cherry, the hollyhock, and the chrysanthemum. It is also suggested that each of these knots had a symbolical or magical meaning, and also that knots were used long before family crests appear on ceremonial apparel.

1 Savoy. 2 Wake (Ormond. 3 Heneage. 4 Lacy. 5 Dacre. 6 Love. 7 Bowen. 8 Boucher. 9 Stafford.

WALLÉ

Design Techniques before Cloth

If we want to find unusual designs, we must seek for them a little outside the ordinary sources. The methods of creating designs on the surface of material or incorporating design in the construction of material is far older than fabrics woven from filaments spun from such ancient fibers as linen, wool, cotton and silk, far more ancient than the glorious fabrics of Egypt, Persia, Peru and China. The most ancient examples of resist dyeing or batik have been saved for us in the ancient pottery found in the ruined cities of the Indus Valley, Mohenjo-Daro, Harrappa or Chandru-Daro, or in the fabulous grave sites of Peru or Central America. It is from these earlier ceramic designs that modern artists should seek for inspiration for the printed fabrics of today.

If we return to the original source of expression, we will meet again the arts in their early vigor and directness. Man has used the surface of his own skin as a medium of expression and the painting and tattooing of the human body are perhaps among the oldest forms of expression. Here again, whether in the primitive people of northern Britain, whom the Romans called "Picts," or "Painted People," or in the people of the Polynesian Islands, artists of today may find designs to relieve textiles from monotony.

In studying the arts of Africa, which have had such a powerful influence on the spirit of modern design, we should remember that these people at a very early date were in contact with caravans of the Arabian and Hindu traders who crossed Africa from the Red Sea, and introduced into Africa many of the arts now practiced by the native tribes, and also the cultivation of cotton. The later Arab traders were Mohammedans, and no doubt their customers in central Africa were much impressed by their prayer rugs which they attempted to imitate, particularly those made of tufted raffia in pile knot design.

Woven patterns and the techniques of woven cloth appear first in basketry and matting, and stamping and painting is ancient, indeed, on the tapa or bark cloths of the Polynesian Islands. The Gold Tribe of the Amur River in China are famous for their applique of deer skin on their garments made from fish skins. Originality is not something that the artists think up in neurotic dreams. It is a re-interpretation into modern life of vigorous forms of primitive arts where design was something more than pattern and was concerned with the symbolism of the universe as men then understood it and as artists expressed it.

Africa

Marquesas
Islands

England 45 A.D.

Chanhu-daro

Costa Rica

Persia

Tapa Cloth

Africa

Northern China

The Primitive Artist and the Modern Designer

When this illustration was published in October, 1919, the South Sea Islands were still the land of romance and illusion. Outside of our museums, few people knew anything of their arts. Since then, these islands became a reality of rain-soaked jungles and insect pests, and Banzai charges. These isles of mystery are now the names of American victories and the symbols of our sacrifice.

These islands are peopled by many races. Some of them from Southern China and India we know as Malays; a people with a distinguished civilization. The Papuan, or the "frizzy heads," and the Pigmy Negritos belong to the lesser races of primitive people. But each of these people had a distinct art of their own and one that we are now beginning to appreciate.

This illustration includes carvings from war clubs and paddles and decorated shields and the amazing masks from the Solomon Islands. Among these people the artist who could establish relationships with the cosmic powers and the spirit world was as highly honored as the war chief. Modern art needs the stimulus of vigorous primitive forms. Modern art is a Renaissance of primitive art in the terms of today.

Modes and Manners of the Head Hunters of Davao

The wild tribes of Davao, District of Mindanao in the Philippine Islands, have preserved for us some of the most interesting of textile processes, and types of garments which must have had their original expression somewhere on the mainland of Asia, and in remote times.

The warrior with the bolo and shield, the central figure of the illustration, is dressed in a blouse and shorts made of a native hemp and by a process of warp tie and dye fabric or ikat. Even his shield is decorated with carvings into which lime has been rubbed. He wears chains of beads of silver and brass about his neck, and variety in texture is added by mixing small pieces of cork with the beads.

Some of the blouses are as simple in form as those pictured on ancient Grecian urns, and these are made of cotton; one of them is decorated with an applique of colored cloth, sewn in a geometric pattern about the lower edge, the cuffs, the shoulders and the sleeves. Others, which are carefully tailored, seem to follow the early pattern of Arabic or Persian dress, and were introduced by the Mohammedans in the 14th and 15th Centuries.

The arts of these people are remkarable, since they reflect, not only the influence of many past arts, but also the ingenuity of people using simple and available material to create a rich art of fabric and apparel.

The South Seas and Modern Art

Fashion recognizes the vigorous primitive arts of the South Seas as an inspiration for modern design. But, when this page was first reproduced in 1922, only a few of our more creative artists in the textile field had vision enough to realize that here lay a great treasure house of inspiration.

In the sketch, we have illustrated the etched bark girdles of New Guinea; the tapas of Polynesia; the grass skirts of Hawaii; the masks of the Solomon Islands, and the carved cremonial paddles of Samoa. The decades before us will see an even greater interest in these forms of expression.

Tapa — the Mother of Paper and Printing

Every tropical jungle in the world produces cloth made from the pounded bark of trees, principally the paper mulberry. The richest source of this art comes from the Polynesian Islands of the Pacific: Samoa, Hawaii and the Fiji Islands. Here, we find primitive design in its purest form and most vigorous expression. It is more modern than any art we call modern. It is a vivid expression of a primitive people's reaction to ornament and environment. Its techniques include stamping from various forms of carved wood, or heavy cords sewn in patterns on bark, crude stencils and direct painting.

The Arts of the South Seas

The arts of the South Seas show what primitive art meant to people when it was part of their lives, an essential element in their beliefs, when it connected them with the unseen power of the universe.

Although these islands were at first visited only by a few early explorers the romance of their traditions and designs captivated the imagination of the western world. With the prevalent use of air travel and the fine documentary photography of today the arts of these distant lands have become increasingly familiar, and the character and freshness of the designs make them sympathetic in feeling to what we call modern design.

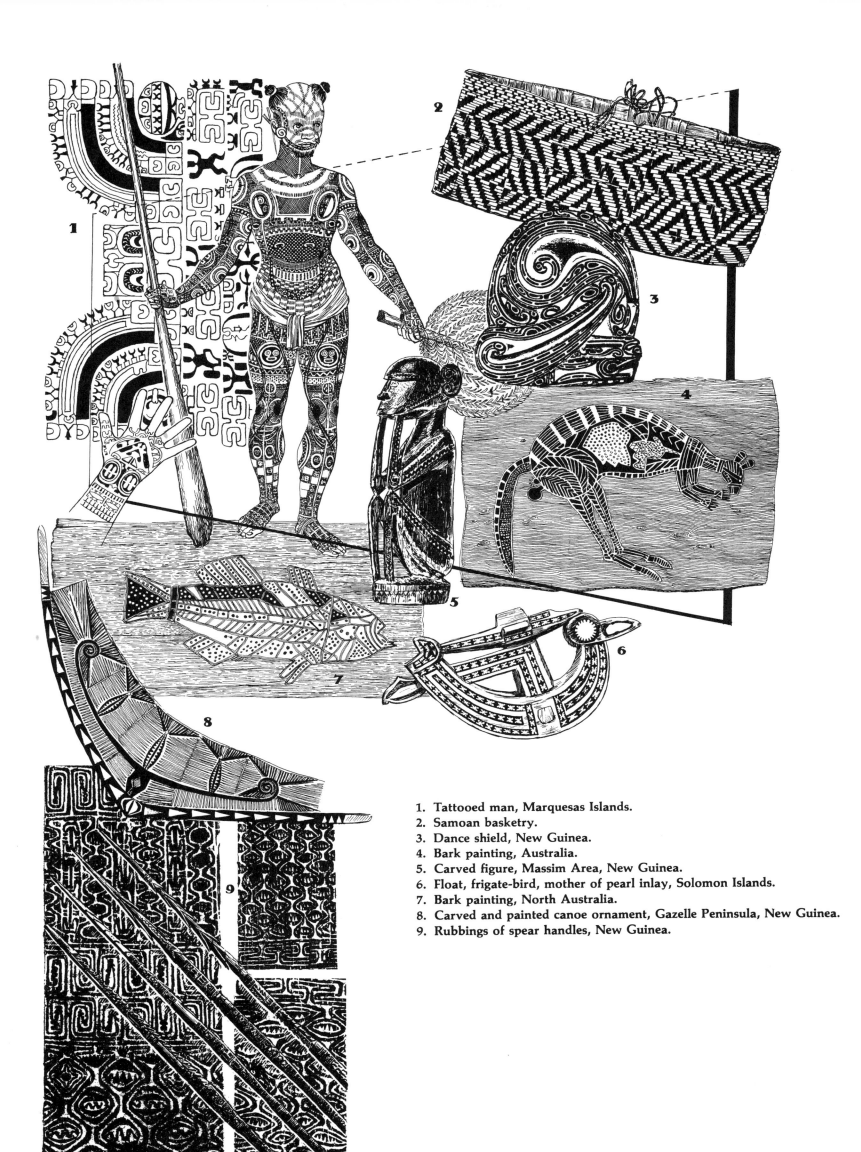

1. Tattooed man, Marquesas Islands.
2. Samoan basketry.
3. Dance shield, New Guinea.
4. Bark painting, Australia.
5. Carved figure, Massim Area, New Guinea.
6. Float, frigate-bird, mother of pearl inlay, Solomon Islands.
7. Bark painting, North Australia.
8. Carved and painted canoe ornament, Gazelle Peninsula, New Guinea.
9. Rubbings of spear handles, New Guinea.

Lace and its Ancestry — an Art and a Great Necessity

Lace making is an art more ancient than the weaving of cloth. It begins with the making of fish nets and snares and carrying baskets. Many primitive people have created interesting forms and patterns in this technique, and left us a heritage of stimulating designs. Here art grew from necessities.

Two master weavers of antiquity, the Copts of Egypt, and the inhabitants of pre-historic Peru, were also skilled lace makers. Their designs have for us today a peculiar interest. They are several centuries older than any of the orthodox lace patterns, but they are more modern in feeling of design.

Lace making today involves the most eleaborate of all textile machines. But, the art of lace making is still a craft and from craft ages we should seek our inspiration.

1. Valiente Indians. Modern Panama.
2. Valiente Indians. Modern Panama.
3. Papago carrying basket. Modern Southwest.
4. Ancient Peruvian lace.
5. Ancient Peruvian lace.
6. 16th Century Italian lace.
7. Ancient Peruvian lace.

8. Ancient Peruvian lace.
9. Coptic lace bag, Egypt; 4th Century A.D.
10. Coptic lace bag, Egypt; 4th Century A.D.
11. Coptic lace hat, Egypt; 4th Century A.D.
12. Ancient Peruvian hairnet or bag.
13. Valiente Indian bag. Modern Panama.

All Hats Are Crowns and All Crowns Were Hats

At the exhibition of the Retail and Millinery Association of America in 1919, *Women's Wear Daily*, through the courtesy of the American Museum of Natural History and the Brooklyn Museum, presented an interesting exhibition of hats from various parts of the world and from various times. These hats represent the great civilization of China, Bokhara, and Japan, and the folk arts of Africa, the islands of the Pacific, Russia, Norway, Sweden and the Koryak tribe of Northeastern Siberia. These illustrations suggest that all peoples have the greatest interest in their headwear and that from all ages suggestions may be taken for modern millinery.

WALE

AFRICA

CHINA 1

4 BOKARHA

5 AFRICA

6 CELEBES

7 CHINA

3 CHINA

8 JAPAN

9 NORWAY 10 PHILLIPINE 11 AFRICA 12 RUSSIA 13 PHILIPINE 14 KORYAH 15 INDIAN 16 JAPAN 17 PHILLIPI 18 SWEDEN

Headwear Types to which
Modern Millinery Owes Much Inspiration

Millinery, seemingly the most fragile and the most irrational of the costume arts, has, nonetheless, a long and a varied history, and is governed by great traditions. All peoples recognize the importance of the hat as a covering and as an ornament for the head.

The illustration includes the hats of simple folk from many lands. There are hats from Central and Northern Africa; peasant hats of Europe; hats from the Northwest coast of Alaska, and the colorful uplands of Mexico. Each of these hats bears a close relationship to the appropriate costume types, and each is expressed in materials found close at hand; and, each reflects the esthetic demands of its own environment and the skills of its creators.

TOP: American 1880, North African Skull Cap, American 1850, French
       1870.
CENTER: American Evening Cap 1860, Huichal Medicine Man, African.
   BELOW: Northwest Coast, Korean Dancer's Hat, Belgian Congo Chief-
       tan's Cap, French Peasant Bonnet 1890.

Sandals, Moccasins and Boots

Man did not ride or drive into civilization — he walked.

Until man began to invent footwear, he could not begin to be civilized. The invention of sandals, moccasins, boots, shoes, etc., are, in reality, the first chapter in the great drama of transportation and travel. Sleds and wagons, horses, camels, oxen and reindeer represent the second phase of this story, and created demands for other types of footwear. At first, man was his only beast of burden, and he had to have the proper kind of footwear before he could start. It is the story of the sandal and the moccasin and their combination.

We present this illustration more as a suggestion of the possibilities of research in this field than as a complete coverage of this vital subject.

1. An Apache moccasin. The long tongue-like insert is usually painted and frequently bordered by beaded bands. The pattern is used as a background.

2. A square-toed, black leather shoe, found in excavations in Windmill Street, London. Late 15th Century. A similar shape was in use in armor at the same period.

3. Broad-toed English shoe of the early 16th Century.

4. Worn by the Belgic-Britons in the early 14th Century, made of cowhide.

5. Southwest Indian boot made of elk's skin painted in turquoise, brick red, gold and dark blue.

6. Hand-tooled leather sandal from Ceylon.

6-A. A sketch shows detail drawing of folded leather strap.

7. Southwest Indian moccasin cut of one piece of chamois. Pattern is used as a background.

8. Shoes worn in England in the 16th Century. Velvet was used for the upper classes and leather for the poorer people.

9. 17th Century English shoe worn by Lady Stafford, of bright yellow brocade embroidered in floral designs with crimson silk and green wire.

10. Shoe of Queen Elizabeth of England, made of ribbed salmon colored silk, embroidered in silver and crimson, with lining of dark red leather.

11. Leather sandal from Southern India studded with silver on the ankle straps and also down the center of the sole.

12. An all-wooden sandal from India.

12-A. Shows the interesting way the solid wooden heel and toe are cut out.

13. Brown leather moccasin from the Eastern woodlands appliqued in bright colors and heavily beaded. The pattern is used as a background.

14. Chinese children's shoe made in brilliant colors.

15. Heavily tooled brown leather sandal from India with wooden heel and toe. The nob has a red top with gold band.

16. Reddish brown leather sandal from Arabia. Handstitched in natural colored cotton.

17. Moccasin worn by the Plains Indians, decorated with fringe and bead work.

History in Shoes — Fashion in Footwear

The American designers of footwear have long made use of historic material, and this is one of the reasons why American shoes lead the world of fashion. Our designers are not only skilled technicians, but they know the history of shoes and how to use this knowledge in their creative efforts.

Footwear was one of the great industrial arts of the Middle Ages, boot and shoe makers, cobblers, tanners and curriers were formed in guilds, and each guild had its own armorial insignia. The handcraft shoemakers of today still use the same types of tools known in Europe from the 18th Century down to modern times. Most shoes are made today by precise and accurate machines. But, the designers of today are studying the technical skills and the artistic knowledge of the past in order to bring greater interest and charm to the footwear of today. The machine has become a tool of precision.

1. Nobleman's shoe, 8th Century, A.D.
2. Pointed or poulaine shoe, 15th Century.
3. Military shoe, soft leather, 15th Century.
4. Man's soft shoes, laced up the front, 15th Century.
5. Man's slipper boot, 1851.
6. Clogs for wear over woman's velvet slippers, 18th Century.
7. Men's leather shoes, English, about 1700 A.D.
8. Woman's silk damask shoes, English, reign of George II.
9. Postillion's boot, English, 18th Century.
10. Deerskin boots worn by Henry VI of England, 15th Century.
11. Soft shoe, or slipper for city wear, French, 17th Century.
12. Shoe belonging to Pope Leon III, 9th Century.
13. Soft boot of a French nobleman in the suite of Anne of Austria, Wife of Louis XIII of France, 17th Century.
14. Slipper of Henry III of France, 16th Century.
15. Soft shoe of German townsman, 16th Century.
16. Soft shoe of a French gentleman of the 16th Century.
17. Lady's laced boot, 1851.
18. Buckled boot, French, 18th Century.
19. Man's soft shoe with lace "Wings," French, 17th Century.

Art in Footwear

The Elizabeth Day McCormick collection was rich in examples of the finest and most extravagant footwear since the days of Cleopatra and the fabled courts of Persia.

At the upper left, two attractive versions of the high tongue front, the upper one taken from the first half of the 18th Century, in a fabric shoe with allover cross stitching covering the surface, red piping, a red leather heel.

Below it, antique green satin from 1750 with antique silver embroidery, a neat strap closure. Above, one of the novelties, a chased silver tip protecting a red velvet mule type from dusty streets, and an attractive white-embroidered fine black kid oxford with pink and blue flowers.

Three interesting sole arrangements, chiefly designed in early days to wear over shoes and protect them, in the manner of our present overshoes, are sketched at lower left, also from the Elizabeth Day McCormick Collection.

At top center, delicate green brocade attaches the shaped sole to the foot; there is a tiny "step" into which the heel of the shoe fits, and the leather which supports the patten is stitched in a design. The second has what we would call today a walled last and interestingly suggests our present-day play shoes, with its heart-shaped vamp cut out, its crossed straps and side walls holding in the heel. Again, there is the step to fit the shoe heel into. This is black leather.

Another version of the idea appears at the lower left, with a squared-off forepart and articulated sole, the heel supported in the sole by means of a metal cup.

Two clog versions at the right include one from 1640, at the top, in white perforated leather with delicate pink tassels, and an X-strapped vamp in brown leather. This is an extremely elaborate type, as is the patten below it, a tongue oxford tie in gold satin featuring a straw-like design, green laced through tassels, and the interesting flat protective sole in another interpretation, this time attached to the shoe.

Historic Footwear Yields Design Ideas

All of man's necessary changes in costume, due to subsequent inventions, are reflected in his footwear.

Primitive people have a way of covering the structural lines of their clothes with ornaments and, at a very early stage, ornamental footwear made its appearance. The jeweled sandals worn by the luxurious ladies of the early Roman Empire were decorated with the priceless Oriental pearls for which, until the 19th Century, no imitations were available. The wealthy classes of Europe, during the Middle Ages, made shoes of the fabulous brocades of the Orient, and from the looms of Venice and Genoa, and wore stilt-like pattens of wood to lift them above the mud and filth of the medieval cities. These stilt-like platform shoes were worn as late as the 18th Century and even in colonial America. During the Empire Period in France, in an effort to imitate the Greek and Roman fashions of that time, delicate slippers of satin were worn, so fragile as only to last for a single promenade, and costing enormous sums.

Fashion, while always new, moves, nonetheless, within the pattern of tradition. Each century has alternative vogues for the pointed, and the square or rounded toe. The use of brocades and satins, of embroidered jewels and tinsel yarn fabric is, by no means, new. We do not imitate the fashions of yesterday, but they inspire the fashion life of each today.

Fashion, in time, becomes costume history, and this history, in time, inspires the new fashions. It is an endless and fascinating cycle.

1740

1812

1780

1812

1890

1880

1913

1923

1923

1920

1913

1900

1912

The Anatomy of Fashion

Our civilization is composed of the unity of many peoples and many cultures from all over the world, and from all of these arts and cultures we draw heavily in our own composite civilization. The Anatomy of Fashion proves that the history of fashion is in turn composed of the creative efforts of many people working out their own problems in their own environment, and exchanged through trade. The history of fashion establishes beyond question the unity of the human race, since all ages and all peoples have contributed to fashion, and all fashions of all times may be an inspiration for each or any new season and for all peoples.

The costumes of people, in various parts of the world, are broadly determined by their physical necessities, conditioned, in turn, by the opportunities, the limitations and the genius which occur in various environments. Tailored clothes, made originally of furs and skins of herd animals by the use of the eyed needle, flow gradually and directly among the Arctic cultures of northern Asia and America from the earlier inventions of the European Ice Age 20,000 to 40,000 years ago, when the eyed needle and the button were invented. But the draped costume of early China, India, Mesopotamia and the valley of the Nile was conditioned by the incandescent heat of these regions. The absence of herd animals to furnish them with skins, and the presence of certain textile materials, such as silk, wool, cotton and flax, led them to the invention of cloth. Most of the costumes of Europe today are the result of a combination of these two factors, for, through all human relationships, from the earliest times down to today, run the nourishing currents of barter, and, ultimately, trade or commerce for monetary profits. In the exchange of invention, there is a vast fertility of ideas and the fruitful combination of ideas.

This is the key to the history of fashion and other human arts, from an historical point of view. But, there is a basic human necessity for ornament, no matter whether people are contending with the withering cold or the incandescent heat in their environment; whether they are restricted to the use of pelts of animals or the products of looms and needlework, there is still the desire for decoration to emphasize the dignity and importance of the individual and to place him in the proper relationship to society, and to answer the esthetic yearnings which are a part of all human nature. Hence, a large amount of the energy necessary to produce clothes is expended in decorating clothes, in the mysterious influence we know today under the somewhat ephemeral name of fashion. Even people who wear no clothes at all are affected by this same powerful human hunger, and there are fashions in body painting, tattooing, just as there are in fabrics, ornaments and silhouettes in clothes.

All over the world, and through all times, men have been affected by the structure and the essential functions of the human body, and fashion is forced to divide itself into functional types of creative invention in garments.

Greenland

Bokara

China

Japan

Pueblo Indian

France

Persia

Plains Indian

Huanam Islands

Czecho slovakia

Spain

France

American

African

English

French

Persian

Brittany

The Blouses of Many Lands as an Inspiration for Fashion

The blouse, the bolero, the poncho, the tunic and the huipil are all names from different areas of the world for the upper part of feminine apparel. In the illustration we attempted to show the many types of necklines, sleeve insets, and types of decoration which various peoples in various times in the history of the world have used for this type of garment. The illustration includes the Alaskan raincoat of seals' bladders and the Eskimo hooded jacket of sealskin which has special interest at this time, since it furnished, with other garments from the North, the model for the uniforms worn by our Arctic aviators. At the seams in the Alaskan raincoat, feathers were sewn both as decoration, and also, to lead the water away from the seams.

We call particular attention to the Philippine blouse with design in appliqued cloth, a rare blouse from San Salvador, a tapestry poncho from old Peru, and the peculiar tie in the blouse from Northern China.

Russia.

India.

Korea.

Central America.

Peru.

New Mexico.

Spain.

Plains Indian.

Persia.

Alaska.

Northern China.

Peru.

Philippines.

Guatemala.

Eskimo.

Indian.

San Salvador.

WALÉ

Around the World in Blouses.

Indian Costume and Fabric Art
Reflects 5,000 Years and More of Invasions

Cotton and the intricate technique of resist and mordant dyeing and the arts of the draped costume are the gracious gifts to civilization of ancient India. The statues of Buddha and the way the women of the Indian courts still wear their gossamer saris remain for us classical examples of the costume arts.

Silk, tinsel yarns, tailoring and embroidery came into India from time to time from the North and West with the Mohammedan invasions. In the remote past, the ancient Hindu merchants carried these techniques and this merchandise to the ports of the Red Sea, the Eastern Coast of Africa and the islands of the Indian Ocean, and the Mohammedan conquests of the 7th Century spread them from Spain to China. Western European ocean born trade of the 16th Century carried these ideas in many forms all over the civilized world.

East Meets West in Russia —
Constantinople, China, Persia

Russian civilization and Russian art stands midway between the West and the East; midway between the past and the present. On one side, it touches Baltic Europe; on the other, the civilizations of central Asia and China, while one of her richest culture streams stems from the great city of Constantinople, now Istanbul, the last bulwark of classical culture and of the ancient and gracious arts of the Near East. In her arts, we find not only the vigorous and direct expression of a new people rising to the status of civilization, but also the memories of arts that were old when Greece herself was a new maritime power in the Mediterranean Sea, with branch colonial ports of trade on the shores of the Caspian Sea.

The Russian still wears his blouse over his trousers, and he tucks his trousers into his boots. One side of his nature is touched by the cultures of western Europe and the Mediterranean, but the other side is influenced by the ancient East, through his contacts with Central Asia and China. Russian art shows all of these influences molded into an art which is distinctly Russian.

Russian Art — A Mosaic of the Centuries

Early in the 17th Century, Russia began her expansion across Asia in much the same way, as a century later, our forefathers poured into the great West. In this march of colonization, they came in contact with the most ancient form of tailored costume in all history: the fur garment of Northeastern Siberia, and the forms of armor once worn by the hard-riders of Genghis Kahn.

The second figure from the last, on the right side of the bottom line, is a Koryak costume. It is designed for winters, in which temperatures of sixty degrees below zero are not uncommon. It is from this and related costumes among our Eskimos that our Northern aviators derived their uniforms during World War I. The decoration is a mosaic of fur, set in geometric patterns, with additional embroidered designs made from sinews.

The central figure on the bottom line represents a woman of the Kirghiz tribe. Her jewels of silver and semi-precious stones recall the contacts of these people with many of the civilized areas of Central Asia. It may come as a surprise to learn that the tribes of Northeastern Siberia, living under the most rigorous winter conditions in the world, not only design their apparel to meet these conditions, but expend a great amount of ingenuity and energy in decoration.

Fashion is a more powerful influence than the bitter cold of the frozen tundras.

A Costume Designer Walks through a Museum

A stroll through any great museum collection brings a fashion artist in contact with many fresh ideas for modern costumes. This page first appeared in *Women's Wear Daily* in 1922 to illustrate the ideas that came to an artist walking through the Metropolitan Museum of Art one morning. She sketched European wall paintings, Persian tiles, a 19th Century American doll, a Chinese statue of Buddha, and the portrait of a 17th Century Flemish dowager. From these original ideas, she created this group of costumes and materials in the mode of 1922.

India Conquers Her Conquerors

India has known many conquerors. For ages, invading armies have streamed through the northern passes onto the rich plains of India. But each conquest has added some new product, some new art to the cultural wealth of this ancient land. Persia and Asia Minor contributed wool, a rich color palette and tinsel yarn. China, Burma and Central Asia contributed silk. From the north came tailored costumes. In the central parts there is a mixture of tailoring and draping; and from the south, we have the purest of all draped forms and cotton at its most exquisite loveliness.

India accepted her conquerors and conquered their arts. These matters are clearly defined for us in the ancient stone carvings of her temples, and in her illuminated miniatures illustrated by Persian and Indian artists, depicting scenes of the court life of her rulers. But India has left another record in the arts which Western Europe borrowed from her and on which they established their own sense of design, color and texture.

These fashion drawings of 1919 were inspired by the arts of India but expressed in the terms of the early 20th Century in America.

The East Brings Gifts of Beauty to the West

The costumes grouped around the throne in the upper half of the illustration are from the original documents from the Oriental collections in the Brooklyn Museum. The five sketches at the bottom of the page express a fashion artist's idea of interpretation in the year 1919.

Oriental costume art represents not only the distinct creations of India, Persia, Central Asia, and China, but the results of contacts between all these people through thousands of years of trade, migration, and conquests. European costume, since the Crusades, has been powerfully influenced by the arts of the Near East and India.

Le Coq d'Or and Costume Adaptations

Le Coq d'Or, as presented by the Metropolitan Opera in the early Twenties, was a brilliant musical and costume success, and had a great effect on the fashion designs of that period. But, the theatrical artists did not have to create these fantasies. They found them almost in the form in which they presented them in the history of the Russian courts of the 16th and 17th Centuries.

Under Peter the Great, Russia began her career of greatness, and this was reflected in the sumptuous and brilliant costumes of his court.

Modern costume is often influenced by the stage, but the stage, in turn, often takes its inspiration from the history of the past.

Yugoslavia — A Brave People Bravely Costumed

Yugoslavia met the onrush of the Nazi Army as she had met the invading armies of the past, with courage and determination and a will that accepted disaster but refused disgrace. Ever since Constantinople fell in the year 1452, Mohammedan armies have invaded Europe through the Balkans. It is a story of rapine and disaster, of privation and suffering, and of devoted courage. These invading armies left behind them the traces of those gracious arts of the Near East, which still find expression in the folk arts of this gallant people.

The foreground of the plate illustrates how a fashion artist in 1921 interpreted this splendid material.

Spanish Art: Half Oriental, Half Occidental

No period in the world's history in which men think deeply and live richly can help but seek the fertile field of Spanish art for suggestions of artistic expression. Half Oriental, half Occidental, but always vivid with life and color through all the vicissitudes of history, these people have retained their keen delight in an unqualified emphasis of fine color and romantic mental vision. Spain may suffer poverty, may see her armies defeated, her insane ambition crushed, but the heart of the Spanish artist knows no defeat, and the glory that once lay like a mantle on the Spanish throne has never been taken from the lives of the Spanish peasants.

Velasquez, Goya and Zuloaga, separated by centuries of time, would have understood and appreciated each other.

Latin America is filled with the relics of a loveliness brought to her by the cavaliers of old Spain. The vigorous independence of her republics has never for an instant diminished her sympathetic and romantic interest in the arts and the history of the peoples from which they sprang, and it is a glorious history: the red courage of old Spain flashed like a comet over the steaming jungles, above the barriers of the impassible mountains, and when the vigor of her armies was forgotten, the beauty of her artists lived and mingled with the native loveliness.

It is a tribute that will quickly be appreciated if our artists in costume and fabric pay fealty to the arts that are interwoven into the very lives of these people.

Old Spain Adds Color to the Fashions of 1919

Spain, in the 16th and 17th Centuries, had a rich and vigorous art. On the one hand, she touched the culture of France and Flanders, but also took richly from the Near East and Moorish inspiration.

The upper scene represents Spain in the days of the caballero, of Cortez, Albuquerque, and Philip II. In every season of rich color and texture, Spanish influence makes itself felt. The sketches below indicate the richness of costume which followed the end of World War I as interpreted by Ruth Reeves.

RUTH.
REEVES.

Spain Brings Gifts to the New World

The Spaniards introduced into the New World, in the 16th Century, the horse, the bull and sheep; iron and steel, and the idea of the tailored silhouette. The skilled craftsmen of Latin America accepted these rich gifts and incorporated them in their own folk arts.

1. Curaca festival costume, Peru, 16th Cent. Hat of silver.
2. Woman's costume from Cuzco, Peru.
3. Gaucho costume, 1840, Argentina.
4. Woman's costume from Otavalo, Eduador.
5. Silver ornament from the region of Lake Titicaca.
6. Characteristic colonial Spanish headdress, Cuzco, Peru.
7. Mounted figure of the Magi, Bogota, Columbia.

8. Peasant woman's costume from region of Cuzco, Peru.
9. Leather belt from Paraguay with silver ornament; worn by Gauchos.
10. Woman's dress from Cuzco, Peru.
11. Ceramic bull as shown in the festival of Pucara, Peru.
12. Woman's costume of the Huancane Tribe, Puno, Peru.
13. Hat, Cuzco, Peru. The part fitting the head is crocheted.

A Peasant Wedding in Sweden

Scandinavia has a rich tradition of the arts which were originally practiced in the Near East and around the Black Sea. Many of these forms of expression were the aftermath of the Mohammedan invasions of Eastern Europe, in the 16th and 17th Centuries. But, there is an even older tradition which associates many of the designs and techniques with those adventurers who came up the Volga, the Dnieper, and the Danube, and established contacts between the Baltic, the Mediterranean, and the Black Sea even before the Christian era.

In the festival lives of the peasants, especially in their marriage customs, these colorful costumes survive. Sweden, like other Scandinavian nations, realized their value and worthiness, and has preserved them in special museums, and by assembling actual peasant villages and encouraging peasant industry.

Peasant Art in the Brooklyn Museum

After World War I, Stewart Culin, then Curator of the Brooklyn Museum, felt that the social changes which were inevitable in postwar Europe would destroy the great peasant arts of Central Europe. He went to Central Europe and made the greatest collection of peasant arts gathered in America, and perhaps in the world. This plate was inspired by some of the material he brought back to the Brooklyn Museum at that time. These folk arts are still an inspiration to costume and fabric designers.

Peasant or folk art is a reflection of the contacts of the peoples of Eastern Europe with the arts of the Near East.

Yesterday in Italy: Fashion Inspirations of Tomorrow

Italy was once the roadway through which many of the arts and philosophies of the Near and Far East penetrated into and enriched the arts of Europe. The peasant arts of Italy, as of other nations, contain many of the rich traditions of the past, when the upper and more mercurial classes had abandoned them for some passing whim of the moment. In Italy, we find reminiscences of the great mercantile cultures and civilizations of Sidon and Tyre which, under King Hiram, 2000 B.C., were the great centers of international trade in luxuries. When the Greek merchant mariners took over the trade of Phoenicia, many of the cities of Italy were founded as emporiums of this trade. The later vigorous industrial trade cities of Italy were closely identified with that great capital of the eastern Roman Empire, Constantinople. Italy also had contact with the vigorous child of Phoenicia, the great city of Carthage. She drew from the rich Arabic civilization in Sicily, and later from the vigorous arts introduced by the Norman conquerors at the time of the Crusades. She felt the impact of the French Revolution and the era of Napoleon.

The great silk industries of France, and the less important one of central Europe, were originally copied from and inspired by the arts of Milan, Venice and Genoa. Her peasant arts are still a living museum of many brilliant yesterdays.

Greek Meets Greek from Crete to Marathon

The Greeks from the time of Homer, the Fields of Marathon and the Pass of Thermopylae have left us not only a history of devoted courage, but also an example of a shrewd race of navigators and traders who sailed on the Mediterranean Sea, through the Bosporus to the Black Sea and the land of the Golden Fleece.

The Greeks of today have inherited this courage. They stood almost alone before the invading German armies. They were defeated; they were not conquered. In the arts of modern Greece, there is a rich inheritance of the Greeks of Asia Minor, of Persia, the Aegean Islands and of the Seljuk Turks. Folk arts keep alive the past and inspire the future.

Chartres Cathedral
Inspires Costume Design

Chartres Cathedral, finished in the year 1260, is not only one of the world's greatest achievements in architecture but its richly sculptured ornament is still an inspiration to the costume designer.

Chartres was completed in the century of Marco Polo, the traveler, and Genghis Khan, the great Mongol ruler, who protected the caravan routes of central Asia from China to the Mediterranean, and brought the products of China and India and of the Mongols in abundance to Europe.

China and India, in their statues of Buddha, illustrate the gracious arts of draping. But the Mongol horsemen contributed a suggestion of tailoring, and also the use of quilted fabrics in which silk floss was used for padding. The combination of these arts is reflected in the carving on Chartres.

Modern designers still find inspiration in this material.

CHARTRES   CHINESE   CHARTRES

Fashion Sketches in Brass, 13th to 16th Century

One of the most accurate records of the costumes in England between the 13th and 16th Centuries is to be found among the life-size brass etchings which were placed above the tombs of the nobility during these centuries. Here we find the draped costume of the 13th Century, and the knight in link armor, the beginning of plate armor in the early 15th Century, the influence that this had on both men's and women's costumes and the time of Queen Elizabeth, when trade with the Orient was beginning to affect the styles of England.

These are actual contemporaneous fashion drawings of these interesting centuries. Few of the original costumes remain, and, if it were not for the four thousand such etchings, scattered all over England, we would have no clear understanding of what the costumes had been in these periods.

These early brasses were once called "cullen plate" because the brass was imported from Cologne on the Rhine. In the latter part of the 16th Century brass foundries were set up in England to supply this demand.

WILLIAM BAYNE

The Elegants of the 15th Century

Contemporaneous records of the earlier centuries of the costume history in Europe are scanty — rare illuminated manuscripts; stained glass; the royal seals and the carven facades of cathedrals, and fragments of fabrics in the treasure rooms of religious institutions. But, the finest of all records are the early Gothic tapestries of Flanders and France. The material for this plate was taken from Demotte's "La Tapisserie Gothique," one of the most carefully prepared of art histories from the early Renaissance.

This plate deals with the great 15th Century. By that time, the Italian cities of Genoa, Florence and Venice had not only developed a trade with the Near East, but had organized their own industries of fashion and had acquired, to some degree, the arts and skills of Asia Minor and Syria. Wealth had increased in Europe, and the influence of the Crusades had reached its zenith. The courts of Flanders, France, and even of England, were centers of trade and luxury, wealth and elegance.

"La Tapisserie Gothique" is one of the great treasure houses of design, both for fabric and for costume, including millinery. It is a wise designer who turns, from time to time, back to original sources.

The Trouser throughout History

Protective covering for the legs begins with the sewn trousers of the Ice Age, but, as these ancient hunters spread across the Steppes of Asia, they domesticated the reindeer, the camel and the horse, and their entire economy revoled around riding. They, therefore, developed the trousers of the Ice Age into the perfect riding garment of the Mongols. In other words, the physical necessity of their life, which depended on riding, had definitely determined their type of garment, as the Ice Age had determined its original form. The Mongol and Turkish tribes of Central Asia, whom the Greeks called Scythians, the Romans, Huns, and the Chinese, Hiung-Nu or Horse Archers, lived on the Steppes of Central Asia, following their herds from one pasture to another, and protecting themselves from famine and drought by their constant movement.

After hundreds of years of Mongolian invasions, the Chinese rulers decided that the time for appeasement was past, deciding to fight the nomads in their own country. They became horse archers and adopted not only the horse, but also the Mongolian horsemen's costume.

Trousers are found among certain of the Indonesian people in the islands of the Pacific as far away even as the mountains of the Philippine Islands. Trousers had been introduced into these regions by the latest wave of immigration into the islands from the continent, and the last immigrants had been definitely Mongoloid in type and had brought with them their national costumes. Certain types of trousers, however, found in these islands, particularly those of Java, are more distinctly reminiscent of the Chinese type, and may have come into the islands with the Chinese merchants of the Han Dynasty, or about the first century preceding the Christian Era, or even earlier.

There is some evidence of the beginning of trousers among the North American Indians south of the true Arctic. Our Plains and Woodland Indians wore breechclouts and leggings, attached by straps to the waist, and high moccasins, and a combination of these garments is an obvious transitional form to trousers, which were not introduced, however, until the European invasion which brought with it also the horse and the necessity for trousers.

Trousers begin in Europe with some form of legging of cloth or leather, held around the lower calf of the leg by spiral wrappings. This useful form has survived in the puttee of the soldier. When chain armor was introduced from the Near East into Europe, perhaps by the Vikings, the legs were covered with knitted tights to protect them from contact with the metal mesh. The earliest form of this garment was found in the Danish bog graves of the Bronze Age, and is contemporaneous with the introduction of the horse culture into Europe or about 3500 B.C.

The introduction of heavy plate armor in the 14th Century led to the necessity of articulating this rigid material at the joints and, therefore, the introduction of knee breeches or culottes. With the invention of the musket the value of armor dimished, and its restrictive influence on men's clothing subsided, but the upper classes still retained the knee breeches or culottes and, in the 17th and 18th Centuries, they became the actual symbol of the upper class costume. The revolutionists of France, in the late 18th Century, were known to the upper classes by the derisive term of sans-culotte or without breeches or, in other words, the class that wore the pantaloon.

The knee breeches of the 17th and 18th Centuries were often made of silk, skin-tight, and required very skillful and expensive tailoring to give the necessary fit. Having become a symbol of aristocracy, they were dangerously unfashionable during the French Revolution. Knee breeches were also a part of the uniform of the monarchial armies of Europe, but it was impossible to make enough knee breeches for the rising armies of the Republic of France, and the pantaloon was, therefore, borrowed from the peasant and became, not only the uniform of the conquering armies of the French revolutionary period, but the very symbol of the new freedom of France. Nothing shocked the emigres more on their return to France, after the Restoration of the French monarchy in 1815, than to see apparently well dressed men on the streets of Paris wearing pantaloons rather than knee breeches. The pantaloon of 1830-1840 was tight fitting down to the ankle. Modern trousers made their appearance after the Civil War where, again, military necessity had impelled people to accept the more simply fashioned and more comfortable pantaloons we know today.

Siberian

Scythian

Persian

Persian

Norman

Peasant

Chinese

Turkish

Saxon

17th Century

1790

19th Century

18th Century

Philippine

Paris Begins her Reign of Fashion

Paris in the reign of Louis XIV, late 17th Century, became the political and economic center of Europe, and the flow of taxes to the industries of France put the bankers of this city in a favorable position in the money markets of the world. Anyone who was seeking special favors of government, opportunities to do business in France, had to pay tribute to the powers of money for which Paris was the mecca.

Everything of a political or social nature was centered in the elegant court of Versailles, and the nobles were induced to leave the power, independence and responsibility of their provincial estates and live the elegant and idle court life, which is so famous in song and story. Wherever there is elegance in the world, it still reflects the glitter of Versailles. A successful effort was made in this court to produce the most fantastic series of social ceremonies and pageants the world has ever known since the court of Constantinople.

Toward the end of this century, the rising merchants of New York, Boston and Philadelphia were importing Paris fashions, and the rich brocades, velvets and the gold lace of Lyons were well known to the planations of Virginia and the Carolinas. The luxury of the court of Louis XIV was reflected across the Atlantic on the shores of the New World. Paris had begun a reign of fashion which has lasted for almost three centuries.

CHARLES 1st.

1625

1633

1693

1621

LOUIS XIV

1660

HENRI IV

1630

The 17th Century

The 17th Century in Europe was an era of sudden wealth, the result of the voyages of discovery, trade and piracy of the vigorous 16th Century. Spain, England, France and Holland, bursting with national life, were building their great colonial empires. The royal courts were centers of luxury and extravagance, and a rising class of wealthy merchants and shrewd professional men vied with them in splendor. It is recorded that Louis XIV wore a be-jeweled costume, including diamond buttons, which cost over 2,000,000 francs.

Lyons was replacing the Italian cities as the center of luxury silks, and Paris had replaced Venice as the home of fashion. The great Cardinal Richelieu, and his follower, Mazarin, and even Louis XIV himself contended vainly against the spread of fabulous luxuries because they believed that so much money spent in markets outside of France would undermine the local economy. The lower classes and the peasants were unaffected by this luxury, and lived in the abject misery which, ultimately, led to the French Revolution. In 1660, on the 17th of November, Louis XIV, at his great minister Colbert's dictation, signed an edict against the wearing of foreign laces. The well-dressed nobles and merchants of France protested so vigorously that Colbert induced Dame Gilbert d'Alencon to bring in twenty Venetian lace makers and two hundred Flemish workers, and workers, and established them with a substantial subsidy, in the Faubourg de St. Antoine in Paris to make laces.

This vogue for lace continued until 1790 and the rise of the Revolution. Armor had become largely ornamental, due to the increased effectiveness of gun powder and the use of the musket, and man's costume was no longer controlled by the rigid lines of armor worn for real protection. The knight had given place to the engineer in warfare. The tailor was freed from the armorer.

There was a larger use of all kinds of cosmetics than there was interest in personal cleanliness. There was more silk than soap. But it was, nonetheless, a great age of fashion, and one of the best illustrated by contemporaneous engravings. This age has left many details still of value to our designers.

MARIE DE MEDICI

Watteau — Father of French Fashions

The father and the inspiration of French fashions was Jean Antoine Watteau, the son of a modest coppersmith of Valenciennes, who first sketched the vivid life of the strolling players and montebanks in his native provincial city. He came to Paris as a youth at the dawn of the 18th Century, and there was powerfully influenced by the stirring birth of fashion and elegance in the French capital.

Watteau found in the gay life of the theater and the colorful pageant of fashionable life the inspiration for his paintings and decorative drawings. Like all good artists, he idealized and emphasized what he saw. His works, gaining fame by their allure and delicacy, in turn inspired the "Marchands des Modes," and the designers of fabrics and accessories. Watteau's pictures reflected the ebullient life about him, and this life took in turn its form, color and detail from his reflections of it. Every period of charm and elegance since that remote time until now has had its touch of Watteau. The fashions he painted were distinguished by simplicity and restraint in head-dresses and by gowns which fell in voluminous folds of cloth at the back directly from the shoulders. Many of the styles which are usually referred to as Watteau belong to the creations of his imitators and followers. These we have illustrated in the central area of the sketch, by way of contrast, which show, not only more elaborate and sumptuous fabrics, but, also, a greater extravagance in coiffure and in hats.

Watteau was followed in popularity and influence by the artists Fragonard and Nattier, and by the works of his own pupils, Boucher, Lancret, Chardin and De Troy.

The city of Lyons was just coming into royal prominence as a center of fabric design and elegance and was finding world markets for the fabric design and elegance and was finding world markets for the fabrics which led to the Jacquard loom work of the early 19th Century and our own times.

Every time we think of elegance in apparel, we naturally think of Watteau who, more than any single individual, may be referred to as "The Father of French Fashions."

A Fabulous Decade of Fashion, 1778 — 1787

The Gallerie des Modes et Costumes Francais, 1778-1787, covering the first decade of the reign of Marie Antoinette, is the most complete history of a decade of fashion which exists in the world. The young queen was the central figure in a fashion pageant which lasted until the dawn of the Revolution.

It was an age of fantastic unreality, and the woman was concealed in an effort to express the artificial, if gay, social pattern of the court of Versailles, where twenty thousand members of the French nobility lived in and on the court. Men's costumes were no less extraordinary than the women's. Embroidered coats and skin tight satin knee breeches and elaborate wigs were worn by the nobility. The court costumes were regulated by strict rules of etiquette. But, in the daytime costumes certain liberties were allowed and the beauties of the French court dressed as shepherdesses with short skirts of painted silks and calicos and with soft corsets, rather than stiff whalebone stays and rich brocades of court ceremonies.

The millinery represented the utmost in artificiality and technical skill. The French fashions of the 18th Century were accepted in every court in the world, including Colonial America, and even in the costumes of the children and in the French theatre.

Fabrics of Luxury — Aprons of Fashion

The fabrics in the Elizabeth Day McCormick collection represent some of the finest examples of the textile arts of France and England during the 17th and 18th Centuries. France had borrowed the draw-loom from the Italian textile centers, and had developed her own silk culture. Early in the 18th Century, Lyons became the world center for silk and tinsel fabrics of luxury, and northern France for printed webs.

The brocade at the top of the illustration is a late 17th or early 18th Century woven design. It illustrates an artistic treatment of the pineapple, a fruit recently borrowed from the New World. The second brocade dates from the middle of the 18th Century and represents the realistic treatment of flowers, which was the distinguishing characteristic of French textile design of this period.

The third is a silk painted in China in Indian designs. The fourth is a madder print made from an etched copper plate. Both of these fabrics belong in the era of Marie Antoinette.

The first apron is embroidered in the characteristic French flowers of the time; the second is a copy in tinsel yarn and colored silk of the embroidered patterns usually associated with the Greek Islands. The apron was not alone a feature of English fashions of the 18th Century, but came to be recognized as a work of art.

Directoire and Empire Periods

The French Revolution drove from France the gilded society of brilliant and frivolous Versailles, the nobility and rich financiers, and the life of regulated luxury and extravagance of the Old Regime. There had been a bitter civil war in Lyons, and the old industry of silk had been destroyed. Gone were the heavy tinsel brocades of the court costume and the dainty fabrics of the shepherdesses, which still survive for us in the Dresden china figurines. Those who had been the leaders of Fashion were driven from Paris; but Fashion herself stayed in her ancient haunts changing her modes to fit the thoughts of the new and turbulent age — the Directoire and the Empire.

It became the fashion to wear the gossamer silks of the East and the delicate cotton muslins of India, because Napoleon was ambitious to conquer the Orient by the road Alexander the Great had once traveled. Fashion now revealed the form and the younger women dressed like Greek goddesses while the more mature adopted the more discreet silhouette of the Roman matron. There was simplicity; but there was also extravagance, for these costumes were embroidered in threads of gold and real jewels were worn. It has been said that the silk slippers copied from ancient sandals, only lasted for one promenade on the avenue. Men also abandoned the tight-fitting knee breeches, once the distinguishing mark of the well-dressed gentleman, and adopted the more democratic trousers. The costumes of the lady of fashion of this era cost as much or more than when Marie Antoinette was queen.

The Restoration Looks to the Court

By 1830, the Restoration was in full swing, and the Republican simplicity of the Empire had become definitely unfashionable. The wasp-waist had been lowered; the sleeves and skirts were fuller, and the bonnets had taken on something of the fascinating trivialities of the late 18th Century. The men are still wearing the Republican pantaloons, but had returned to the skin-tight breeches in their riding habits. The only thing that has survived from the time of Napoleon is the cashmere shawl, worn by the central figure in the bottom row, and it is no longer a real cashmere, but has become a paisley, made on a European loom.

Victorian Fashions — England and France

The age of Victoria in England was the age of Eugenie in France, and, in both countries, there was a strong social effort to make the royal courts centers of fashion, and to compress fashion into the rigid mold of court etiquette. The wasp-waist, the rigid bodice and the hooped skirt all suggest the influence of the 18th Century and glittering Versailles. Court fashions were used to increase demand for merchandise.

"Grandma's" Fashions

By 1875 the United States and Europe had recovered from the depression of 1873, and an age of inflation prosperity had begun. Dressmaking in this decade had lost its sense of discipline and tradition. The vast amount of accessories and fabrics were made by machine methods of mass production. The audience which wore expensive clothes had been vastly increased by the new riches which poured into the development of steel mills, the growth of the railroads and the petroleum industry.

It is, perhaps, the most drab and absurd period in costume history, but the dressmakers had still retained a reminiscence of needle skills. At the end of this period the silhouette had evidently been modified with some reference to the necessity of railway travel. The dressmaker had become largely the selling agencies for the vastly increased production of fabrics due to the increase of power-driven machinery. There was all the extravagance of old Versailles with little of its charm.

Canadian Arts and French Heritage

Until the year 1763, Canada was a French Colony and the Jesuit priests and the fur traders had reached as far west as the Rocky Mountains. There was a series of French forts stretching from Quebec to New Orleans, down the Valley of the Ohio and the Mississippi, connecting them in one pattern of commerce and political power.

The early French settlers brought with them, not only the gracious arts of 16th Century France, but also the peasant costumes of Normandy and Brittany. The Algonquin and Iroquois Indians borrowed French motifs for their bead work and the courier de bois took something from Europe but more from the Indians in their characteristic costume. Here we have an interesting relation of arts from both the New and the Old World and a brilliant source of costume and fabric inspiration.

The peasant costumes shown in this plate are still worn in provincial France on festival days.

Colonial Latin America

The Spanish conquest of the rich primitive civilizations of Latin America brought in to contact two great arts: those which had originated and developed in the Americas, and those which Spain had inherited from the Near East during the period of Mohammedan invasion. Under the direction of Spanish masters, in the 16th Century, the native craftsmen built and decorated churches and palaces, and created jewelry, fabrics and ceramics in the Spanish style, but added to each some touch of their own skills and their own perceptions of design. In this way, a rich folk art has grown up among our southern neighbors, in which there are combined the great skills of both the Old and New World, and the high esthetic values of two different cultural systems.

1. Silver pin from Lake Titicaca, Bolivia.
2. Araucanian iron bit inlaid with silver, Chile.
3. Colonial knitted glove from Peru.
4. Araucanian silver figurines from Chile.
5. Two-piece woman's costume from Guatemala.
6. Ayacucho bull from Peru.
7. The Avenging Angel of silver filigree, Lima, Peru.
8. Woman's costume from Chola, Bolivia.
9. Pottery plate from Guanajuato, Mexico, 1839.
10. Silver basket from the coast of Peru.

Bird Forms in Magic and in Art from Many Regions

The arts of pre-Columbian America are recognized today as not only among the great arts of all time, but as a specially appropriate source of inspiration for American creative efforts.

In all primitive arts, bird forms are among the most frequent inspiration. The bird plays a leading role in all mythology, and artists all over the world and in all ages have created bird forms in an endless and fruitful variety. Each art grows from some previous artist's expression, and the designers of today will find the bird forms, as expressed in the stone carvings, pottery and the fabrics of our early Americans, a rich and almost untouched source of inspiration.

We have selected our material from the ceramics, stone carvings and fabrics of Peru, Central America, Mexico and the Southwest and the Indians of Michigan.

Fabric Design and Ceramic Art

Only in recent years have a few museums recognized the ceramics of Central America as a part of the history of the fine arts of the world. There is a close relationship between the arts of pottery and the arts of fabric design. In many parts of the world they are interchangeable, and one art powerfully affects and stimulates the other.

In Central America, particularly in Costa Rica, few fabrics have been preserved because of the dampness of the climate, but their ceramics, so richly represented in our great museums today, give us some idea of what the fabrics themselves must have been in the past. We have taken a few samples of the patterned pottery and have used the designs with little, if any, change to show how they might appear on modern fabrics.

Rain in Fashion Imagination

All people in all ages and climes have sought protection from the rain. The natives of the west coast of Africa cover their bodies with castor oil and pigments of red ochre. The natives of the jungles of the Amazon and the Orinoco smear themselves with turtle oil and the juice of the bixa or orellana which gives them a red coloring. These primitive cosmetics protect the wearers from evil spirits, from insects and from chilling winds and rain falling on otherwise naked bodies. The primitive inhabitants of the Arctic region turned their fur garments skin side out in the rain, and the Aleut Eskimos make a hooded poncho from the split intestines of seals, at the seams of which feathers or furs are inserted both for decoration and to prevent leaks. The natives of the rice-growing countries such as China, Japan, Java, Korea, the Philippine Islands, etc., make cloaks of rice straw and huge hats in the form of baskets. Among the maritime people of the low countries, England and Brittany, the people wear heavy fabrics of coarse native wool from which the lanolin has not been entirely removed. The early stage coach drivers created garments of many capes for protection. The mercantile riders, who carried the wares of Italy into the markets of Europe in the 16th Century, evolved costumes from similar types of fabrics. The natives of the Polynesian Islands of the Pacific cover their tapa or bark cloths with a vegetable resin which sheds water. In the jungles of South America the Spanish conquerors became acquainted with the juice of the rubber tree, latex, and learned to smear it on their garments to protect them from the almost constant tropical rains.

As early as 1819 a Scotchman, named Charles Mackintosh, joined two pieces of cloth together with a core of rubber — the famous Mackintosh. In our Civil War, the demand for water-proof clothing, blankets and ponchos was so great, the rubber industries of this country had an enormous development.

Around 1840, Charles Goodyear evolved a mixture of rubber with sulphur which made vulcanized rubber possible. This process made it possible to keep rubber from melting except at high temperatures and from becoming stiff and unwearable in the cold. The Gauchos of the Argentine took advantage of the closely woven native fabrics to furnish themselves with ponchos which gave them protection from the storms of the pampas. The gentleman of the early 19th Century adapted the formal military cloak intended to protect the solider from the weather and turned it into one of the most luxurious of men's garments.

The women of the 19th Century also depended on heavy woolen garments as a protection against the rain. But, as early as 1875, waterproof capes of gossamer cloth, coated Scotish gingham or boiled silk, giving the appearance of rich black silk, were advertised that could be rolled and carried in the pocket of a coat.

We are still trying to protect outselves from the rigors of the wind and the rain. We still have the same problems, but we solve them in the laboratory with physics and chemistry and not by nature and accident.

China

Italy

New Guinea

Korea

Mexico

Philippines

1875

1834

Eskimo

France

1802

Argentina

The Spirit of the Nineties

In the period of the 1890's a number of our most extravagantly dressed women, the leaders of society in New York, Philadelphia, Washington, Lenox and Newport, had their clothes made in Paris and were the customers of the couture of that period. Models were brought to the United States and copied line for line, and detail for detail, by our dressmaking establishments. This was almost a generation before the opening of the ready-to-wear dress industry in this city. It was the age in which the piece goods and dressmaking supply departments in our great retail stores were principal centers of fashion. The copies made in this country were as like the French originals, as it was possible for ingenuity and skill to make them. It was the age of the rustling and ruffled taffeta petticoat, of light colored broacades and satins, of laces, velvets and embroideries. It was the age of great and intricate dressmaking skills, and the mills of France produced a whole series of new and complex fabrics and decorative details dear to the feminine fancies of that time. It was the age in which New York society was composed of the famous four hundred names.

Among the great names of this period in Paris was Frederick Worth, the Englishman who had established himself in Paris in the age of the Empress Eugenie, and whose descendants are still among the fashion creators of Paris. The three costumes illustrated in the lower part of the sketch were all created by Worth. He inspired many of the fabric designs which the mills executed to his order.

This age of extravagance, self-indulgence, ostentation and artificiality reveals, nonetheless, an interesting phase in the long history of costume design, and one which should be carefully studied by designers of today.

Sports of the 19th Century

The modern world of sports was born in the century of our illustration and with it the obvious need for special costume involving comfort and function for new activity. We may think of our world today as being much more sports conscious than the 19th Century but there are fewer new sports than old sports activities which have died out during the first half of the 20th Century, among these, diablo, shuttercock and battledore, and croquet which is played much less by adults. It might be said that skiing has replaced tobogganing, sports cars and bicycling, that swimming and beach sports have increased tremendously and of course flying has since become a mode of transportation.

In costume the most obvious change is in skirt length and general quantity of clothing as in the skating costume, the yachting, archery and bowling attire. Horseback-riding has become predominately astride, exchanging skirts for pants, as both golf and tennis exchange skirts for shorts.

Fashion in our Greatest Century of Invention

This illustration outlines the fashion changes in men's and women's costumes for a hundred years or between the dates of 1820-1920. This century includes some of the greatest technical and mechanical changes man encompassed in a century, and, consequently, some of the most far reaching social changes in human history. It includes the development of the steam engine, the steam boat and the railroad; the development of electricity from a cabinet wonder to a faithful servant; the telegraph and telephone, ocean cable and other industries; the development of chemistry in dyes, processes and synthetic fibers. In the cycle of fashion, to which this illustration refers, we must consider the introduction of power driven automatic machinery in the textile industry, and the sewing machine and various other machines used in the production of ready-to-wear clothing. But, of greater influence on our lives and fashions was the evolution of our system of interchangeable parts, serial production by automatic machines, which brought innumerable forms of wealth. In 1820, the verb "to manufacture" still contained a trace of its original Latin root, meaning to make by hand. Now, it means an intricate coordination of machines, a continual flow of mechanical movement which results in finished products of the greatest precision. We have achieved the golden age, the era of super-abundance.

The best dressed man or woman of any period, detached from his surroundings, would look either quaint or ridiculous. The beauty of Helen of Troy and Cleopatra, which changed the currents of history, or the fabulous creatures of the court of Versailles, if they appeared at a night club today would be mistaken for cosmetic publicity stunts. Louis XIV once wore a jewel embroidered costume which cost two million francs, and Beau Brummel was a sensation in fashionable Bath. If they should wander into the Waldorf today, they'd be mistaken for over-dressed door men. Timeliness is the essence of fashion.

The way people live, their furniture, homes, methods of transportation, all must harmonize to create fashion. The fashions of the sexes must compliment each other. If fashions for women change, men's must follow. Neither sex can ever dress for themselves alone.

If our age is to really enjoy Fashion, we must harmonize all the various influences that are at work. Costume designers must know something of furniture, ceramics, and what kind of homes our people want, and what they do. Fashion is not just a new trick in silhouette, color or design. It is a pattern of living, a philosophy of life.

In all fashion, there must be a relationship to the events and aspirations of the moment, but also a memory of the past. It is a continuous sequence of change revolving around the axis of events. Its objective is to bring into harmony the various environments which mankind creates and controls. Fashion is a way and pattern of living controlled by various other forces, but, in the end, bringing these forces into focus and balance.

Historic Costume and the French Couture

From the time of Louis XIV down to our own days, the city of Paris has been the center of fashion for women. One reason for this early success was that Paris recognized the enormous value of historic costumes as a source of inspiration for modern design. As late as 1920, she established another museum of historical costumes for the benefit of her designers. This museum had had an exhibition of ancient costumes in the Louvre in 1909 but was not formally opened until January 24, 1920. The object of this association was not only the preservation of ideas for archaeological studies leading to the understanding and reconstruction of the ancient costumes, but also for the inspiration of modern designers.

LOUIS XIII.

LOUIS XIV.

LOUIS XV.

CHARLES IX.

ALderman of Nuremberg.

La Grande Couture, 1900 — 1906

Paris has an uninterrupted tradition of international dressmaking from the 18th Century down to the end of World War II. There are legends of Rose Bertin, who was the favored milliner and dressmaker of Marie Antoinette. But, the grand couture, we were to know, begins in Paris in the late half of the 19th Century, and during the reign of Napoleon III and the Empress Eugenie.

The costumes shown in this illustration are in the first decade of the 20th century. Paris, at that time, was the center of fashion, for the entire world, and well-dressed women from New York, London, Vienna, Cairo, Bucharest, Buenos Aires, Rio de Janeiro, and even the courts of Japan and India, came, each season, to her salons for their apparel. It was the age of elegance, the age of fabulous luxury; of great skills and low wages, and a limited and artificial field of fashion.

All these costumes were worn by the divas of the French theatre of this period.

Georgette

Martial et Armand

NEWFIRM   REDFERN   Dœuillet

ROUFF

ERNEST RAUDNITZ   WORTH

The Bandboxes of New England—Containers of Charm

In the Orient, the container was often the work of art. This was also true of our 19th Century bandboxes. In those days, whoever brought home a new bonnet had a permanent treasure in the box. These boxes are now collected by various museums and are rich in their inspirational value to modern fabric designers.

The majority of the designs shown in the sketch were taken from bandboxes in the Cooper Union Museum of Arts and Decoration.

New Bedford—Her Cotton Mills and her Whalers

New Bedford, Massachusetts, the great whaling center of the 19th Century, was, at one time, the most important fine yarn cotton town in America. She sold her goods in the gray, and had no interest in fashion. Her first mills were built to give employment to the wives and daughters of her whaling seamen who visited the ports of the Orient on their voyages.

In 1921, when New Bedford had begun to feel her lack of style, *Women's Wear Daily* published these designs to show what cotton in New Bedford might have been.

No industry ever can be greater than its inspiration; and no inspiration can rise above the source from which it springs.

Whaling Captains and Textile Arts

In New Bedford, once the center of the fine cotton industry in America, there is a delightful little museum The Dartmouth Society dedicated to the romantic history of whaling. For almost two hundred years New Bedford's sailors visited the ports of the Seven Seas, and the museum is a treasure house of the arts of the Orient and the fabulous islands of the Pacific.

Had the mills of New Bedford only known it, these works of art suggested in this illustration of Indian designs were a richer cargo than the oil and the whalebone and the ambergris they once brought home.

Puritan Ideas in the Fashions of the Twenties

Even Puritan New England Felt the urge of 17th Century luxury and elegance. A century of ocean-born commerce with the Orient had brought to western Europe a sense of rich color and texture in fabrics. Wealth had vastly increased and had spread beyond the narrow limits of the past. Here lies the dawn of modern fashion. Here is a constant source of new fashions.

The First Ancestors of New England and their Arts

The Indians who once inhabited New England have disappeared, leaving only as a memory the names of New England rivers and towns. Some traces, however, of their arts still exist in our museums. They made containers of birch bark, and some of these were stencilled with designs and others had an applique of colored bark. They also borrowed designs from the French and the English and expressed them in bead work. These arts are an almost untouched field for the modern fabric designer.

Persian Art Comes to Pennsylvania

The Germans who came to the colony of Pennsylvania in the late 17th and early 18th Centuries brought with them, not only a desire for independence and the right of religious freedom, but also the folk arts which had matured in Southern Germany, inspired by the arts of the Near East, particularly Persia. In their pottery and fractur paintings, we catch glimpses of simplified Iranian forms. The tulip, which was the symbol of love in Persia, both the plant and the design, came into Europe in the 16th Century from the Near East and was brought to Pennsylvania in the 17th and 18th Centuries. The arts of the Pennsylvania "Dutch" are among the treasures of museum collections.

Painted Decoration on Chest

Sgraffito Pie Plate

Slip-Decorated Dish

Sgraffito Pie Plate

Fractur Painting

Art in India — Cotton in America

The most ancient of all cottons come from India, and from India we have inherited the most gracious arts that have ever been expressed in this fiber. Modern machines were invented in England and in the United States, and in time, our southern states produced more cotton lint than any other part of the world. But India still remains the gracious source of art in cotton, and Indian calicoes are not only objects of art in our great museums, but an endless source of inspiration.

In this illustration, we have attempted to suggest not only the arts and techniques of ancient India and the spinning mule of Samuel Crompton, and the good ship "America" unloading cotton in New Orleans; but, also how Indian ancient arts might inspire modern fabrics and modern costume. Our costume sketches were made by Ruth Reeves in 1921.

Dawn of the "Ready-to-Wear" Industry

The years of 1910-1912 were the period of Worth, Redfern and Callot as leader's of the Grand Couture in Paris. French fashions were accepted in the capitals of the world, where a few wealthy leaders of fashion either wore the French originals or copies that were exact down to the last detail of lace insertion.

All of the material illustrated here came either from London or Paris in the form of photographs or sketches. American fashions were still a problem of the distant future. Since that time fashion has spread far beyond its original boundaries either of creation or acceptance. The period illustrated in the sketch marks the high water mark of the dictatorial influence of the Grand Couture on world fashion, and the dawn of the ready-to-wear industry and a more democratic conception of fashion. In those days fashion was the exclusive privilege of a few extravagant women. Now fashion is a part of the lives of millions of women in every community in America, and the demand for American fashion is reaching beyond our national boundaries into the world markets.

Fashions and War — France

Between the Declaration of War in 1914 in France, and the year 1926, great changes had come in the ideas of people and great changes had been effected in their fashions. The fashions of 1914 were definitely designed for the middle-aged women of social position, and these styles prevailed all during the war. Toward 1919, the skirt had begun to rise, and attempts were made to simplify the silhouette, and to create fashions suitable only for younger women. By 1925-26, this tendency had focused in that short and simple slip-on type of dress which has been the characteristic of fashion ever since.

The fashions of the earlier periods contained fabrics of luxury and extravagance, including many delicate laces. There was an undue emphasis on the details of dressmaking. The fabrics of 1926, while no less extravagant, were simpler in detail and relied on texture and color for their appeal.

It is not difficult to understand the fundamental motives which caused these changes. In periods of peace and stability, fashions are set by older women, who have achieved a certain degree of financial and social stability. But war brings youth to the front. Youth expresses itself in those types of costume which we call "Fashion."

PARIS 1914

Group at Auteuil.

1915 LONDON 1916

Selling chocolates
at Benefit for Belgian Red Cross.

Guests at a fashionable Wedding.

LANVIN
1917

JENNY

1918

DRECOLL

1919
BERNARD

1920
PREMET

1921

1922
PATOU

1923
DŒUILLET

PAQUIN

1925

1926

1924
WORTH

LANVIN   DRECOLL   CHANEL

VIONET   LE LONG   PATOU

153

Fashions and War — United States

In World War I, American designers came into their own. The difficulties of obtaining models from Paris and fabrics from France and England lead to a larger degree of originality in the work of our designers and a greater development in our textile industries. This is one of the definitive periods in the history of the costume and fabric arts in the United States.

There were no priorities on fabrics and no control on prices. Cost of material, workmanship and of costumes rose to fantastic heights. The war had cut us off from German dyes, and our own dye industries were undeveloped until after World War I. But, in spite of this, it was a period of brilliant and flamboyant color. The fabulous price for the silk fiber and the change in silhouette were strong factors in the introduction of rayon fabrics into the markets of fashion. It was also a period in which rich embroideries were used to take the place of French brocades.

Hickson
1914

Lucile
1915

PALM BEACH
Bathing suit
1916

TUXEDO PARK
Skating costume

Henri Bendel
1919

1917

Irene Castle

Red Cross
Field Worker

Red Cross
Motor Corps

National League
for Women's
Service.

Farmerette

A. Beller
& Co.
1918

Jaeckel
1919

Jessie Franklin Turner
1920

Mary Walls
1922

Mme. Frances
1923

Otto Kahn
1924

Edw. L. Mayer
1925

Max Cohen
1926

A Decade of American Fashion

The most fantastic decade of American fashion occurred in those lush years of inflation prosperity which followed World War I. It was a decade in which French fashions and fabrics exercised a dominating influence. It was also an age in which American designers began to assert their own talents in original conceptions, and also in their modifications of French models to suit the rising American taste in apparel.

Edward L. Mayer was the outstanding American designer-producer of that era. These illustrations were taken from his workroom sketches of 1921-1931. They show the changes in silhouette which occurred in that remarkable period and also a strong Parisian influence.

Born in Davenport, Iowa, he worked in Philadelphia for a time, and then manufactured calico wrappers in Chicago, where he became the head of the custom dressmaking department in a great retail store. In 1903, Mr. Mayer came to New York City, to manufacture fashion blouses. Here he became the first designer-manufacturer to produce ready-to-wear dresses of the highest fashion and at the highest prices. His collections included all forms of women's apparel, and his merchandise had a profound influence on the development of the top specialty stores in the country.

1921

1926

1922

Ciré satin
ciré emb.
on chiffon

No. 8030

Black
Satin
Grey & gold
brocade trim
Henna
emb.

1927

Bois de Rose
Georgette

1928

on
lace

1923

Maise
Chiffon
shadow lace
blue
ribbon

No. 1706

1925

No. 600

1924

Black
velvet
silver & tan
emb.

No. 1479

Na 2360

1929

Printed
Chiffon

Plumb colored
velvet

1931

net
eta

1930

The Statue of Buddha and the Designer of Negligees

The negligee, the most intimate of all costumes, permits the designer a greater latitude in silhouette and pattern than any other form of apparel. The negligee is a draped costume, and India was the original home of the draped costume. As the Buddhist religion moved out of India, along the caravan routes of Central Asia and into China, stone carvers, inspired by the Greek tradition, produced a series of gigantic statues of Buddha, wearing the draped costume of India. These artists were master sculptors, and had before them the actual models of these gracious costumes. So, these statues are not only great works of art in themselves, but they are the most authentic record of the draped costume at its highest perfection in dignity and interest.

The designer of negligees could find no greater source of inspiration than the Buddhist statues from the 3rd Century of our era down to the 14th Century in Central Asia, China and Japan.

Renaissance of Fashion, 1942

"Renaissance of Fashion, 1942" was a brilliant attempt on the part of the Metropolitan Museum of Art and a group of fashion experts to present to the American costume industries an acceptable substitute for the models which had formerly come from Paris. Ten of our leading costume designers were asked to express their ideas of modern fashion, derived from the inspiration of the Italian Renaissance, so richly illustrated in the museum's collections. These designers were invited to exhibit by the museum and given ample facilities to study the documents but, each artist expressed his own personality and his own ideas of design.

Preston Remington, Curator of Renaissance and Modern Art, assisted by Tom Lee, created a perfect Renaissance setting and specially designed mannequins for the thirty costumes placed on display. This exhibit remained open to the public for three months and the costumes were donated by the creators to the Metropolitan Museum of Art, as a permanent part of their costume collections.

Omar Kiam

Leslie Morris

Mark Mooring

Fira Benenson

Valentina

Nettie Rosenstein

Jessie Franklin Turner

Renaissance of Fashion, 1942

The designers selected not only motives and decorations in weaving and embroidery and printing derived from and inspired by the Renaissance fabrics, but modified the silhouette of the Renaissance to fit the fashion needs of the day. This collection was brilliantly illustrated and well-publicized, and it unquestionably affected the subsequent styles of America.

This was the first time that a great museum dedicated its principal hall to a demonstration of the arts of contemporaneous dressmaking. It came at a time when our relations with Paris had been disrupted by the fall of that brilliant city, and when designers all over America were seeking guidance and inspiration. Fira Berenson, Wilson Folmar, Sophie Gimbel, Omar Kiam, Mark Mooring, Germaine Monteil, Leslie Morris, Nettie Rosenstein, Berthe Stern Simmons, Jessie Franklin Turner and Valentina were the designers.

Wilson
Folmar

Sophie Gimbel

Omar Kiam

Germaine Monteil

163

Changes in Postwar Fashions

Many important fashion changes came during the decade of 1945-1955. During World War II certain restrictions in material and cut were laid down by the government ruling known as L 85, and when that was lifted the designers responded with enthusiasm to the freedom they had regained.

The wartime short skirt and padded shoulders gave way to the "New Look" silhouette introduced in 1947 by Dior, illustrated in the black suit. A few of the other important fashions include the strapless evening gown; the ballerina length skirt; the sheath; the low cut dress with jacket; the full gathered skirt, small waist and tight bodice made popular by Anne Fogarty; the princess silhouette; the stole in fabric or fur, sometimes long and straight, sometimes shaped; the little short jacket known as the spencer, so popular in the early 19th Century, which has been so well adapted for today.

The sources of inspiration for these fashions are shown in the frames in the background of the illustration.

1775

1787

1865

1844

1801

Lili

Influences and Inspiration in Fashions of a Decade

The informal way of living which has become so prevalent since World War II has brought with it more informal fashions.

The trouser is playing a more important part appearing in many different styles to be worn at home in the evening, for active sports and for general country living.

One of the most important style developments for 1945-1955 was the increasing use of separates providing innumerable combinations of costumes with a comparatively limited wardrobe. This has been a development of a world of tremendously increased travel.

Sweaters, which in the past were associated only with sportswear, have enveloped the entire fashion picture and brought with them knitwear in general. Elaborately decorated and low cut sweaters are worn in the evening and the knit cardigan is worn or thrown about the shoulders from morning until night.

The greatcoats, toppers and box jacket suits were all big fashions of the decade, all providing smart comfort for town and country life as well as travel.

The inspiration of these fashions is shown in the background in the illustration.

Development of Fashion through
Recognition of American Designers

In selecting the outstanding designers in America for the period 1943 through 1966, the authors have used the winners of the Coty American Fashion Critics Award. The Coty Award sponsored by Coty, the cosmetic concern, depends upon a jury composed of fashion editors of New York newspapers, national magazines, and newspaper syndicates. The selection of this jury gives a balanced overview of the period. This award was inaugurated in 1943 to assist in promoting and establishing the identity of the American designer.

The impetus for the organization of this presentation was that many leaders in fashion appreciated the outstanding achievements of the American designer during World War II. The use of American designer names had been encouraged by several fashion editors and merchants.

This annual award has become nationally and internationally known as "Winnie;" a companion piece to the motion picture's "Oscar." The bronze trophy, designed by Malvina Hoffman has been presented to those American designers whose work has had a significant effect on the American woman's selection of apparel. The award winners have included recognized prestige designers and new-comers exemplifying both the classical and non-traditional approach to clothes. This wide range of recognition indicates the awareness of the jury that Fashion reflects modern life just as the arts of architecture, of painting, and of music.

Since the founding of the Coty Award, designers in all categories in American fashion have received the "Winnie." In 1951, a "Return Award" was established for designers who, the jury decided, merited the "Winnie" a second time. In 1956, the "Hall of Fame" award was inaugurated as the "summit" recognition of the contribution of the designer who had won both the "Winnie" and the "Return Award."

The following pages present the winners of the Coty Award. The interpretation of this 1943—1966 period and its reflection in fashion art are evident through a study of these designers.

The authors wish to acknowledge the cooperation of Eleanor Lambert and her staff in releasing the information on the Coty Award winners. They extend their deepest gratitude to Rosalind Synder Ritter, Founder Dean Emeritus of the Fashion Institute of Technology, who has been an inspiration and guide in the revision of this "One World of Fashion". Their appreciation is also given to Dorothy Donley, Professor of Fashion Art and Design of the Fashion Institute of Technology, who illustrated this supplementary section.

"Winnie" and Special Award Winners, 1943-1946

1943   Norman Norell   First Winnie Award Winner
Acclaimed for his innovations. He launched several fundamental trends that have had wide effect upon the entire industry.

1943   John Frederics and Mr. John   Special Award
Cited for his world wide millinery fashions including the famous "Lucky Strike" hat in 1930 and the "Jeep Hat" in 1942.

1943   Lilly Dache   Special Award
Selected for her original ideas contributed to the millinery industry. She gained wide recognition as the designer of safety helmets and turbans for women workers in war plants.

1944   Claire McCardell   Winnie Award
Granted because of her influence on American Fashion. Her clothes were unmistakably distinguished by inventiveness of cut and by inspired use of color and fabrics. She made the "popover" dress famous.

1944   Sally Victor   Special Award
Recognized as the first of the big name milliners to make a popular price line. She received the award for the Ha' pennysailor, the Slice Beret, and the "Freedom Bonnet".

1944   Elizabeth and William Phelps   Special Award
Presented for their skilled craftsmanship, in leather and old metals. They were known for the "saddle bag", for the "postman's bag" and for the evening wear belt bag.

1945   Adrian   Winnie Award
Granted to this noted designer of California who was head designer for Metro-Goldwyn-Mayer. His flair for the dramatic, from the bold-broad-shoulder suits — tapered waistlines to sculptured evening gowns, inspired a new fashion for the American woman.

1945   Tina Lesser   Special Award
Given to this well-known creator of decorative sports and beach wear. For playclothes that were colorful, picturesque and exotic. She was a pacesetter in the field of fabric design and decoration Her Cabana dinner set was an outstanding influence.

1945   Emily Wilkens   Special Award
Chosen as the leader in the Teen Age field of fashion design. She designed wardrobes that understood the dimensions and dreams of adolescents. She recognized the figure problems for this age group and her clothes were flattering and smart. She initiated the young Junior look.

1946   Clare Potter   Winnie Award
Chosen for her sports clothes with their unusual and distinctive color combinations. An ease of cut made her clothes comfortable as well as smart.

1946   Ben Reig (Omar Kiam)   Winnie Award
Recognized for dramatic quality in elegant clothes. He created distinctive daytime and evening wear that were simple in line and yet dressy in effect. The clothes were not highly ornamented, but were beautiful in line, cut and texture.

1946   Vincent Monte Sano   Winnie Award
Cited for the Trench Coat for women, for the short sashed coat, and for coats made of silk satin and white wool fabrics. Expert tailoring, excellent design and fine fabrics made his garments outstanding.

1943   Lilly Daché

John Frederics and

Mr. John 1943

Adrian 1945

Claire McCardell 1944

Norman Norell 1943

Tina Leser 1945

Emily Wilkens 1945

Omar Kiam 1946

Elizabeth and William Phelps 1944

Vincent Monte Sano 1946

Sally Victor 1944

Clare Potter 1946

Award Winners for Outstanding Contributions in Four Major Branches of the Fashion Industry, 1947-1949

The jury of 1947 made its selections from outstanding contributions in the four major branches of the fashion industry:

1. custom dressmaking
2. high bracket wholesale dressmaking
3. medium price wholesale dressmaking
4. junior fashions

1947   Adele Simpson   Winnie Award
Attained because of her outstanding achievement of best design in the moderate price fashion field. She was responsible for such outstanding American fashion trends as the "Pepper Mill" silhouette, "Peg O' My Heart" silhouette and the "Vanity Dress".

1947   Jacob Horowitz   Winnie Award
Presented to this manufacturer of Junior Fashions. In the firm conviction that young people are qualified experts on the clothes they wear, he was a pioneer in the use of young talent. Bearing the "Judy and Jill" label, his clothes were noted for their functional wearability.

1947   Mark-Mooring   Winnie Award
Granted to this designer for made-to-order clothes for Bergdorf Goodman. He was noted for the distinction and restraint with which he handled rich materials.

1947   Nettie Rosenstein   Winnie Award
Recognized as a strong believer in the terms "build and construct" in dress designing. She worked out her exquisite drapery in fabric on a live model. Her seemingly endless variations of the "little black dress" were lauded by the feminine world of fashion.

1948   Hattie Carnegie   Winnie Award
Awarded for her superb sense and for her appreciation of clothes. Garments from her establishment had much of the beauty and elegance of French styles. Her designs were the essence of sophistication.

1948   Esther Dorothy   Special Award
Joseph DeLeo   Special Award
Maximilian   Special Award
Attained by these three designers for their excellence in designing furs with unlimited and creative techniques. Furs were combined with fabric for day and evening wear; furs were interpreted into the designs of two-piece suits; furs were utilized for interesting button treatment; and fur hats were used as a complement for the total look.

1949   Pauline Trigere   Winnie Award
Acclaimed for her originality in fashion design and for her imaginative ideas which have set major fashion trends. The "cocoon cape", the "domino silhouette" and the "strapless" evening gown with bodice of embroidered lace were among her contributions.

1949   Toni Owens   Special Award
Cited for her notable contribution to American fashion in the separates field. Her fresh and youthful designs carried the American girl look. One of her innovations, the sorcery skirt, was an ingenious combination of a long scarf that could be draped six different ways to form a bodice.

1949   David Evins   Special Award
Received for his originality and good taste represented significantly in the shell shoe which contributed greatly to America's leadership in shoe fashions throughout the world.

Adele Simpson 1947

Nettie Rosenstein 1947

Mark Mooring 1947

Jacob Horwitz 1947

Esther Dorothy 1948

Maximilian 1948

Hattie Carnegie 1948

Pauline Trigère 1949

David Evins 1949

De Leo 1948

Toni Owen 1949

"Winnie" and Special Award Winners, 1950-1951

1950   Charles James   Winnie Award
Merited by his original development of an architectural approach to the structural shape of clothes. This had a profound influence on fashion trends on both sides of the Atlantic. Through his invention of the new type of mannequin, he spearheaded a new and important shift in the sizing of wholesale garments. In addition, his adventurous use of color earned the admiration of the fashion world.

1950   Bonnie Cashin   Winnie Award
Chosen for her gay and witty approach to sports and street clothes which brought a new vitality to fashion. Her provocative and surprising use of fabrics, such as sheer coats and tweed aprons; and her adaptation of Oriental fashions for contemporary American use were of outstanding importance.

1950   The Julianellis   Special Award
Granted to this husband and wife team, Charles and Mabel Julianelli. Their high standard of artistry and craftsmanship reflected their creative talent in the design of the naked look in shoes which contained the foot securely.

1950   Nancy Melcher of Vanity Fair   Special Award
Selected for the new excitement and beauty brought to the traditional and highly functional lingerie fashions. She was cited for her original handling of nylon tricot, specifically in the permanently pleated nightgown.

1951   Jane Derby   Winnie Award
Recognized for clothes with a high level of taste projecting youthful elegance. While her street clothes were very simple and understated, the dinner and evening garments were exceedingly sophisticated and glamorous.

1951   Vera Maxwell   Special Award
Granted for her designing of clothes that were casual and well-suited to the kind of American living that revolved between city activities and suburban living. Her use of imported tweeds combined with her high standards of workmanship brought a high degree of recognition to this town and country type garment.

1951   Anne Fogarty   Special Award
Chosen for contributions of a fresh flavor in her charming paper doll silhouette for daytime. Her use of cotton in unusual ways and her fine color sense brought acclaims from both fashion experts and the public. She brought fashion to the junior market with the elegance, simplicity and wearability of her clothes. One of her silhouettes, a tiny waist with bouffant skirt, helped develop the trend toward the use of the crinoline petticoat. She was the forerunner of the modern jump suit.

1951   Sylvia Pedlar of Iris   Special Award
Granted for her contributions to the lingerie field. Known as designer "laureate" of lingerie, she adapted nylon fabric to fashion underwear.

1951   Norman Norell   Return Award
Recognized for his continuing leadership in trends and taste in the field of fashion. The importance of his collection with its advanced thinking of the Empire silhouette, with its subtle color and fabric combinations, and with its exceptional beauty was recognized by the leaders of the fashion world.

1951   Pauline Trigere   Return Award
Merited for her constant contributions to the American fashion field. The distinguished chic and wearability of her winter collection were indications of her outstanding fashion sense. Her wrapped coat silhouettes, her souffle sleeve, and her experimental new cuts achieved a fluid, yet slender silhouette combining rare originality with superb workmanship.

Anne Fogarty 1951

Nancy Melcher 1950

Charles James 1950

Mabel-Charles Julianelli 1950

Bonnie Cashin 1950

Vera Maxwell 1951

Sylvia Pedlar 1951

Jane Derby 1951

Pauline Trigère 1951

Norman Norell 1951

175

"Winnie" and Special Award Winners, 1952-1955

1952   Ben Zuckerman   Winnie Award
Selected for his impressive contribution to the beauty and to the originality of coat and suit fashion. A sense of elegant restraint, the translation of the tailored mode into new terms of richness and color, and a superlative and understanding of the texture and grain of fine fabric were outstanding qualities bringing high achievements to this field of fashion.

1952   Ben Sommers of Capezio   Winnie Award
Recognized for his continuing growing influence on shoe fashions by his adaptation of the soft dancer's shoe, to day and party shoes for women, for children and for men. Working with leading designers, he demonstrated that the ease, the grace, and the perfect comfort of the ballet slipper and of the stage shoe could be turned into functional shoe fashion.

1952   Harvey Berin   Special Award
Presented to Harvey Berin and Karen Start, a perfectly balanced team of manufacturer and designer, who dominated the festive clothes field in America. By producing lusciously pretty clothes at moderate prices, they made the glamorous party dress a standard garment in the wardrobe of thousands of women.

1952   Sydney Wragge   Special Award
Chosen for his feminine sports fashions seen through an artist's eye for line and color executed in direct simple terms. Within the realm of the "sturdy" fabrics, such as grey flannel, silk shirting and tweed, his designs displayed individual distinction.

1953   Thomas F. Brigance   Winnie Award
Awarded for versatility in creative design, for consistant good taste and imagination, and for the sense of adventure in his collections. The simplicity of line and shape and the imaginative use of color and fabric, not only in sportswear, but also in coats and suits, marked him as an outstanding American talent.

1953   John Moore of Talmack   Special Award
Shared by Matty Talmack and her designer John Moore who contributed to the fashion scene by creating exciting clothes of fashion quality at moderate prices. Gay, sophisticated fashions became available to women of middle income levels.

1953   Helen Lee   Special Award
Selected for her significant influence in the development of good taste and charm in children's fashions. The ability to make little girls look dressed up without fussiness, a sense of color in fabric, and a fashion instinct enabled her to do the almost impossible — enchant the mothers and the children too.

1954   James Galanos   Winnie Award
Presented to this California designer whose influence was phenomenal in the fashion field. A flair for the unseemingly simple day dress appropriate for luncheon and for evening and a talent for developing a single silhouette in different fabrics resulted in producing garments that fulfilled a need in the American scene.

1954   Charles James   Special Award
Returned earned recognition for the second time by the Coty Jury for his continuing contributions in the development of designs based on structure in the field of dresses and coats.

1955   Jeanne Campbell   Winnie Award
Noted for the development of fabrics particularly suited to young smart life. The Award was based on her related collections which indicated excellent cut, fine fabrics, and color sense. The clothes reflected the American trends in the inexpensive sport market.

1955   Anne Klein   Winnie Award
Recognized as a young designer who made an outstanding contribution toward making the Junior field a fashion leader market. Designing for the young in figure, but not necessarily young in age, she broadened the appeal and influence of this area.

1955   Herbert Kasper   Winnie Award
Cited as a young designer presenting consistent wordly young elegance of fabric and of cut in clothes for a wide range of needs from casual garments to short evening dresses. His collection reflected the general trends presented in a young but sophisticated fashion.

1955   Adolfo of Emme   Special Award
Attained for originality of design for the fresh use of materials, for unstereotyped ideas and for a particularly charming sense of color in millinery.

John Moore 1953

Harvey Berin 1952

Ben Zuckerman 1952

Sydney Wragge 1952

Helen Lee 1953

Thomas F. Brigance 1953

Ben Sommers of Capezio 1952

James Galanos, 1954

Jeanne Campbell 1955

Herbert Kasper, 1955

Anne Klein, 1955

Charles James, 1954

Adolfo, 1955

Adolfo, 1955

Reflections in Fashion as Influenced by the Cultural Patterns of the 1955-1965 Decade

The cultural patterns of 1955-1965 were influenced by many factors. The decade was one of outstanding technological advances and initiated the space age. The excitement and vitality of exploring new unknown areas was reflected in a fresh look to fashion. Individuals were stimulated to seek the new, the different in fabrics and in design. Then, too, the population explosion resulted in an increase of the youthful market. Manufacturers, retailers, and publishers geared their promotion of fashion toward the teen-ager, the college youth, the career girl, and the young suburbanite. In addition, during this time, Jacqueline Kennedy, a young First Lady with fashion awareness and a feeling of elegance, influenced the taste of American women.

The young look became the keynote of the period. Young designers who had the ability to recognize the interests, needs, and desires of youth became a strong influence in the development of contemporary trends in fashion.

Sports and travel increased tremendously. Vacation periods in various seasons, the jet airplane, and the credit system stimulated all persons to travel more and farther. Participation in sports; such as boating, skiing, surf board riding had become almost universal. These activities promoted research by textile mills for fabrics that were wash and wear, packable, and crease resistant. Designers emphasized co-ordinates and interchange for any activity and for any time of day. Designers were impelled to make provision for the traveler limited to a jet plane. They had to offer clothing designs for those who would water ski in the Mediterranean in the morning and dance under the Oriental moon the same evening, have breakfast in New York and dinner in Istanbul.

The activities of the young in music, dance, painting, and theatre had also given this decade a sense of newness. The folk singers, the Beatles, the electronic beeps, the discotheque, pop art, op art, and theatre of the absurd, promoted amusing and off beat fashion approaches that were adapted to practical designs. The topless bathing suit was presented as an off beat interest and influenced the development of the "nude look." The "beatniks" influenced the designs of sweaters, slacks, and jeans. All clothes developed fluidity, action, ease, and movement. This decade of 1955-1965 became one of the young look reflecting a broad spectrum of activities, interests, and tastes.

"Winnie" and Special Award Winners, 1956-1957

1956   Norman Norell   Hall of Fame Award
Launched as the first winner Hall of Fame Award in recognition of his attainment of an unchallenged world position among fashion designers. His profound influence on the silhouette through more than a decade and his faultless sense in the handling of fabric for its full potential of beauty earned this accolade for him.

1956   Luis Estevez   Winnie Award
Recognized for his outstanding position as a designer in American fashion. Within the framework of current fashion and within a disciplined price range, he created highly individual and imaginative clothes for the young sophisticates of America.

1956   Sally Victor   Winnie Award
Merited because of her leadership and her consistent excellence in the millinery field. She is known for her master stroke of designing which has made the hat an indispensible and irresistible part of the American woman's way of life. Some of the hats which earned this award for her were: her flowered hat and her black and white fur hat.

1956   James Galanos   Return Award
Granted for his creative talent and consistent achievement. He was responsible for many influential fashion trends in the use of materials, such as wool combined with chiffon, indicative of his magnificent sense of fabric.

1956   Gertrude and Robert Goldworm   Special Award
Recognized this mother and son team for leadership in the American Knitwear field. Their outstanding sense of suitability, correctness and good taste combined with their full knowledge of knitting techniques contributed a large share in the development of this industry to a top position of the fashion industry.

1957   Leslie Morris   Winnie Award
Granted to this designer of coutourier clothes in day and evening wear for Bergdorf Goodman. The distinction and elegance of her ball gowns are achieved with luxurious fabrics combined with perfection of detail and workmanship.

1957   Sydney Wragge   Winnie Award
Attained for his imaginative use of fabrics; unusual prints, tweeds, bold plaids and exclusive weaves and textures. Among Wragge "firsts" have been sleeveless dresses, the sophisticated jumper dress, the wool sheath and the short-sleeved side slit coats. He has been the favorite designer of persons living in suburbia.

1957   Emeric Partos   Special Award
Selected for his ingenuity and technical skill in the draping and handling of furs. Associated with Bergdorf Goodman, he designed for the individual customer emphasizing the total look.

Gertrude and Robert
Goldworm 1956

Luis Estevez 1956

Hall of Fame
NORMAN NORELL
1956   1957

James Galanos 1956

Norman Norell 1956

Emeric Partos 1957

Sally Victor 1956

Sydney Wragge 1957

Sally Victor 1956

Leslie Morris 1957

181

Hall of Fame, "Winnie" and Special Award Winners, 1958-1959

1958   Claire McCardell   Hall of Fame Award
Granted posthumuously to this imaginative, creative designer. As *Harper's Bazaar* said of her, "She created a race of clothes inwardly, outwardly in the American grain... they had their roots in our own history, our own psychology. They were related to the frugal modesty and dignity of the dresses of pioneer women, to the stitched and riveted sharpness of our workman's overalls, to the almost abstract garb of our great escape figures of the comics."

1958   Ben Zuckerman   Return Award
Merited by his consistent and brilliant fashion leadership in the field of tailored clothes. His use of the contoured shape in most exciting forms brought vitality and charm to the coat and suit industry. His trend-setting ideas achieved world respect.

1958   Arnold Scaasi   Winnie Award
Awarded for his contribution to the glamour of late day and evening fashions. Using the most deluxe and gay fabrics to enhance the grace of his designs with a technical artistry for ready-to-wear production, he achieved a couturier conception to this clothes.

1958   Donald Brooks   Special Award
Cited as a designer of vital clothes for our young American women. Often first with a fashion idea, he pioneered the relaxed and the high-waisted styles. He was the favorite of the active fashion aware young women who appreciate the razor sharp elegance of his clothes.

1958   Jean Schlumberger   Special Award
Received for restoring imagination and true design conception to the precious jewelry of this period. Veering from the classic type of setting, he transformed the beauties of nature — shell, leaves, butterflies, fish — into jewelry in unique combinations of gems. This broke precedence in contemporary craftsmanship and opened new vistas in the field of jewelry design.

1959   Pauline Trigere   Hall of Fame
Recognized for her instinctive creativeness, a pioneer of many fashions, including capes, reversible coats, and wool evening dresses has proved to the American fashion industry that sophistication and elegance can be achieved by understated styling with emphasis on cut, proportion, color and use of quality fabrics.

1959   James Galanos   Hall of Fame
Presented to this California fashion designer for his continued good taste, sophistication and perfection of design for day, afternoon and evening clothes.

Scaasi 1958

Ben Zuckerman
1958

Jean Schlumberger 1958

Hall of Fame
1958
Claire McCardell

1958   Donald Brooks

Hall of Fame 1958
Pauline Trigère

Hall of Fame 1958
James Galanos

"Winnie" and Special Award Winners, 1960-1962

1960 Ferdinando Sarmi Winnie Award
Given for bringing to American ready-to-wear clothes a couturier conception and execution. That women should look beautiful, particularly in the evening, and, that they should feel the assurance of quality and continuity that make clothes a very personal part of a woman's life were his major aims in designing.

1960 Jacques Tiffeau Winnie Award
Selected for his unique and prolific approach to fashion from two distinct points of view; his designs for Tiffeau-Busch, created within a limited price range yet with style authority and great effectiveness for the young, and his collections for Monte-Sano and Pruzan, designed for the adult and sophisticated woman with a demanding sense of quality and timelessness. To both fields he brought fresh originality and imagination.

1960 Rudi Gernreich Special Award
Received for his knitted bathing suits which influenced the entire world of fashion in swim suits. Through his seemingly endless ingenuity and variety, the Gernreich knitted bathing suit became a symbol of the fashion development of the jet age.

1960 Sol Klein of Nettie Rosenstein Jewelry Special Award
Recognized as an outstanding contributor to the pre-eminence of American costume jewelry in fashion. He brought costume jewelry to a new high standard of quality by his introduction of perfectionist techniques heretofore restricted to the manufacture of precious jewelry.

1960 Roxane of Samuel Winston Special Award
Selected for capturing the contemporary mood for luxury and grandeur in evening fashions. While she was a designer of signal ability in daytime fashions, it was her evening collections of beaded and embroidered dresses which made fashion history.

1961 Ben Zuckerman Hall of Fame Award
Lauded for his continued outstanding contribution to the elegance of the coat and suit. He was considered the maestro of this field as shown by his recognition in two previous years.

1961 Bill Blass Winnie Award
Selected for his variety and flexibility in presenting the elegant clothes that were designed for the wearer to choose according to her personality and appearance. His clothes are ageless and chic. Fashion critics have been extensive in their praise of his collections.

1961 Gustave Tassell Winnie Award
Awarded to this California designer, not only for his couturier collections, but also for his sportswear presentations in the moderate price range. His creations were uncluttered and almost ingenious in their simplicity. They were fashioned of elegant fabrics with emphasis on perfection of workmanship and fit.

1961 Bonnie Cashin Special Award
Granted for her introduction of innovations in the use of leather and of combinations of leather and tweed. She was recognized as one of the outstanding designers in Sportswear in harmony with the needs of current sports

1961 Kenneth of Lilly Daché Special Award
Chosen for his trend-setting hair styles during the year. He was particularly noted as the designer of Mrs. John Kennedy's coiffures which influenced the hair styling of the American woman.

1962 Donald Brooks Winnie Award
Recognized for his versatility in designing an outstanding collection of clothes for wholesale production, an elegant presentation for the coutourier market and the clothes for the theatrical production of "No Strings".

1962 Halston Special Award
Received for his design of hats using all types of fabrics, furs, leathers, beads and feathers. Halston Frowick, known in the industry as Halston, was associated with Bergdorf Goodman.

Halston 1962

Sol Klein 1960

Kenneth 1961

Jacques Tiffeau 1960

Rofane 1960

Ferdinando Sarmi 1960

Bill Blass 1961

1961 Hall of Fame 1961
BEN ZUCKERMAN

Gustave Tassell 1961

Bonnie Caskin 1961

Donald Brooks 1962

Rudi Gernreich 1960

"Winnie" and Special Award Winners, 1963-1964

1963   Bill Blass   Return Award

Presented for visualizing and creating a total look which smart women could wear with elegance. Considered a trend-setter. Has successfully launched into other avenues of the apparel industry, and his designs are understated regardless of age group.

1963   Rudi Gernreich   Return Award

Recognized as a designer of unusual range who created with equal ability and impact anything from a topless bathing suit to an evening costume. This California designer's topless bathing suit inspired a whole field of designing with the "Nude Look".

1963   The Edelmans of Fleming Joffe   Special Award

Cited for their contributions in new uses of leather as a fashion medium. This husband and wife team also initiated specially treated plastics, such as: snakeskins, painted python skins, and black alligator. Name designers were inspired by their unusual treatment of reptile skins.

1963   Betty Yokova for A. Neustadter   Special Award

Chosen because of her use of furs in unusual ways; such as, sable for travel and tailored coats and mink and chinchilla in overblouses.

1964   Geoffrey Beene   Winnie Award
Jacques Tiffeau   Return Award

Received the Return Award and the Winnie recognizing their non-static, non-traditional, witty, imaginative and snappy approach to clothes which were as much a phase of the modern life of the period as Action Painting, Progressive Jazz and Pop Art. Some of Geoffrey Beene's trend-setting designs include longer jackets, seven-eighth length coat costumes and bias cut dresses. Jacques Tiffeau's influence was shown in quilted plastic raincoats, town suits of giant hound's tooth checked wool with wide pleated skirts. Many of his jackets and coats has his well-known stand-up and stand-away neckline. His designs included hoodlike skull caps of matching fabric or fur snoods.

1964   Sylvia Pedlar of Iris   Special Award

Received her second Special Coty Award for her promotion of the revival of grace, beauty and decorativeness in intimate clothing.

1964   David Webb   Special Award

Selected for his brilliant blend of a sculptor's talent with the jeweler's skill and for his interpretation of jewelry in animal forms of gold and jewels. He was known for his animal bracelets made of colored enamel and precious stones.

"Python" by The Edelmans 1963

Rudi Gernreich 1963

Betty Yokova 1963

Bill Blass 1963

David Webb 1964

Sylvia Pedlar 1964

Geoffrey Beene 1964

Jacques Tiffeau 1964

187

Special Awards — New Young Contemporaries, 1965

1965

Nine young contemporaries, Victor Joris, Sylvia de Gay, Bill Smith, Don Simonelli, Deanna Littell, Edie Gladstone, Stanley Herman, Gayle Kirkpatrick and Leo Narducci were cited for their contribution to fashion of 1965 with a special award. They were honored for the new youth movement that emphasized the uninhibited young spirit which rocked the fashion world both here and abroad. This group of young designers was given the joint special award for bringing vitality and originality to moderately-priced ready-to-wear clothes. They also share a strong feeling for sportswear and a desire to do clothes that are contemporary.

1965   Anna Maximilian Potok   Special Return Award

Presented for her excellence in handling fur designs over the years. Her designs represent the ultimate in luxury fur fashion in the United States.

1965   Tzaims Luksus   Special Award

Awarded as an outstanding American fabric creator who both weaves and prints his own designs. His flat water color florals are some of his characteristic designs.

1965   Gertrude Seperack of Warners Slimwear Lingeries   Special Award

Recognized for the famous Body Stocking. She is also responsible for the equally revolutionary Stretch Strap Bra.

1965   Pablo of Elizabeth Arden   Special Award

Won award for eye make-up. He made popular the use of false eyelashes and is responsible for the new ornamental look in unusual eye effects — bejewelled, befeathered and lace-trimmed.

Gertrude Seferian 1965

Fabric by Zarina Laborio 1965

Anna Maximilian Potok 1965

Pablo 1965

Sylvia de Roy 1965

Bill Smith 1965

Deanna Littell 1965

Don Simonelli 1965

Edie Gladstone 1965

Victor Joris 1965

Stanley Herman 1965

Gayle Kirkpatrick 1965

Leo Narducci 1965

Emphasis on the Young, 1966 Coty Award Winners

The 1966 awards continue the emphasis on the young, on the avant-garde, on the go-go activities of the age, and on the mobility of our modern life. The developments in space, the advances in science and technology, and the economic and political direction within this coming decade will shape the future evolution of our fashion forms.

1966   Dominic Winnie Award

Dominic Toubeix — (he never uses his last name professionally). Selected by the committee for his flair for fresh sophisticated clothes. They have a dramatic quality which is partly explained by his early related concerns — art and the theater. A designer of impeccable taste, impeccable cut, he describes his clothes as "young... sophisticated".

1966   Kenneth Jay Lane Special Award

Presented the award for jewelry and "designer of the witty and colorful costume jewelry" which has captured high fashion for this period. His jewels are never self-effacing. He ignores the usual costume techniques, but like a jeweler, he makes his designs in wax, or by carving or twisting the metal. Mr. Lane uses such unlikely media as shells, leather and plastic stems in his costume jewelry designs.

1966   Rudi Gernreich Return Award

Recognized for his original contributions to all areas of fashion. Often described as the "kookiest American designer of major reputation", he is an original among American designers. Rudi Gernreich's naked swimsuits were shown with paste-on stickers of triangles and circles decorating the body. He has created a way of dressing that is distinctive, precedent-shattering and totally American. This is the third time that he has been recognized by the Coty American Fashion Critics.

1966   Geoffrey Beene Return Award

He was cited for his highly original and superlatively worked suits and dresses. He won his first Coty Award in 1964. He is one of the few designers who has mastered the bias cut. His use of fine dressmaking techniques gives his clothes a custom-made look. He designs clothes that are young, but free of gimmickry and gadgetry.

Dominic 19

Dominic 196

Dominic 1966

Kenneth Jay Lane 1966

Geoffrey Beene

Geoffrey Beene 1966

Rudi Gernreich

Rudi Gernreich 1966

WRITTEN BY

MORRIS DE CAMP CRAWFORD, an eminent authority in the field of fabric and apparel design. The late Mr. Crawford was Research Editor for Fairchild Publications for nearly thirty-five years, and a founder of the Museum of Costume Art, Metropolitan Museum of Art. He was also a research associate of the American Museum of Natural History, the Museum of Science and Industry of Chicago, and a trustee of the Textile Museum of the District of Columbia and of the Brooklyn Museum. His other literary works include: *The Heritage of Cotton*, *The Ways of Fashion*, and *The Influence of Invention on Civilization*.

EDITED AND REVISED BY

JOSEPHINE ELLIS WATKINS, Director of Community Resources, Professor of Apparel Design, and Director of the External Impressions Workshop at the Fashion Institute of Technology. Mrs. Watkins is much in demand as a lecturer on fashion, has written articles for several newspapers and *American Girl* Magazine, and served as Consultant for the Fashion Section of the *1966 Random House Dictionary of the English Language*.

BEATRICE ZELIN, Professor of Apparel Design and Assistant Director of Placement at the Fashion Institute of Technology. In the latter capacity, Mrs. Zelin is in close contact with the fashion industry, and serves as Consultant on training programs for young designers. She is co-author of *Designing Apparel Through the Flat Pattern*, has written for *Design Magazine*, and served as Consultant for the Fashion Section of the *1966 Random House Dictionary of the English Language*.

NEW ILLUSTRATIONS BY

DOROTHY DONLEY, Professor of Fashion Art and Design at the Fashion Institute of Technology. Miss Donley was formerly a free-lance fashion illustrator for such publications as *Vogue* and *Women's Wear Daily*.